ANDY MARTELLO'S

HERE'S YOUR HOST!

....

INSIGHTS AND INTERVIEWS WITH GAME SHOW GREATS

BY ANDY MARTELLO

Just A Martello Books
Las Vegas, NV

Andy Martello/Just A Martello Books
andy@andymartello.com

Book cover layout and design by Suzanne Fyhrie Parrott
SuzanneFyhrieParrott.com

Additional design by Cory Anotado

Edited by Amanda Schrader, Mandieland Literary
mandielandliterary.com

Book Layout ©2013 BookDesignTemplates.com

1st edition.
ISBN 978-0-9970456-2-8
Library of Congress Control Number: 2016919770

To game show fans everywhere.

To aspiring hosts, comedians, and live
entertainers of all kinds.

To Mom and Dad, who always supported their crazy son as
he pursued his entertainment dreams and never had a chance
to hear these a single one of these stories.

To the cast and crew of The Price is Right LIVE!
I promise to make every attempt to thank them all by
name in the Special Thanks section of this book.

CHAPTERS

ONE

···

THE NEW GUY

When my headlining show — *Afternoon Comedy Magic Show Starring Spike and Hammer* — came to an end in mid-2010, it was frustrating to say the least since I had quit my day job to dedicate myself to the show. I chose not to rush off and get a day job, but to redouble my efforts to get more entertainment work in Las Vegas.

Vegas is a tough town in which to get noticed. While the types of high profile gigs are better than what I found in my former Chicago home, the opportunities to work are nowhere near as plentiful. Many of the major casinos have contracts with the same handful of vendors, and they are obliged to split the work equally among those vendors. That means that there isn't a lot of motivation for agencies to be busy finding and booking new talent. To make matters worse, *nobody* returns a phone call, an email, or a text message. It's crazy to see such behavior in the so-called Entertainment Capital of the World.

As hard as I was working, it still wasn't my most prosperous of times in show biz. For the first and only time in my marriage, I was relying primarily on my wife's income and our savings. I am certain the situation was taxing on my wife, and it surely contributed to the demise of that marriage which came to an end in the summer of 2011.

Shortly thereafter, I received an e-mail from my former comedy magic show partner directing me to a Craigslist ad for a Las Vegas show that was looking for an announcer and warm-up comedian. Much to my surprise, the show was *The Price is Right LIVE!*

The Price is Right LIVE! is a live stage version of television's iconic game show. It has been running in theaters and casinos across North America for nearly fifteen years, and yet many people are largely unaware of its existence.

TPIRL is as close to the full *Price is Right* experience you can get without being inside the Bob Barker studio at CBS Television City. While it is not televised, people pay to see a wonderfully entertaining 90 minutes of game show madness and excitement with the added benefit of the real possibility to win prizes just for showing up. It is produced by the same company as the forty-five-year-old (and counting!) television program. It features the same sets, music, excitement, and games audiences have been watching on their television sets for generations. Todd

Newton, the show's most regularly booked host, likes to call it the *Greatest Hits of The Price is Right*. I jokingly refer to it as *The Price is Right on Ice*, which is probably why I am merely the announcer and not the host.

One of the major differences between the stage show and its televised counterpart lies within the live show's ability to offer more people a chance to win prizes. We call up new people to "Come on down!" before every game and give out t-shirts or other small prizes to the contestants who don't appear on stage. To make certain everybody has an equal and fair chance to live out their dream of being on *The Price is Right*, we choose all of the contestants completely at random as opposed to the Hollywood show where the producers cherry pick contestants to guarantee the most exciting televised product. In between the games, we give away small "instant winner" prizes to audience members. In an average show, close to fifty people get a chance to play onstage or win a prize just for sitting in their seat. These are fun changes to the traditional format, and it increases the chances for everyone to have fun, experience a touch of television history, and make a game show dream come true.

One other major difference is the size of our prize budget. We aren't supported by millions of advertising dollars, and simply can't offer a new car with every game. Some people are dismayed by this, but when you consider the licensing fees, the salaries for everyone involved with the show (talent, stage hands, crew, production, marketing and management), transportation costs (buses, semi-trucks and trailers, and airfare), equipment, and theater rental, the fact that we still manage to offer and give away high-quality prizes to so many people per show is quite impressive.

What was most remarkable to me was seeing one of the most recognizable shows in entertainment, produced by the largest distributer of television products in the world, placing an ad on Craigslist looking for the next Johnny Olson (Or Rod Roddy, Rich Fields, or George Gray).

I was already familiar with the live show. Having vacationed in Las Vegas several times prior to moving here, my wife and I had often considered checking out the show, but never did. I won't lie, I doubted the ad was real, but I was so hopeful it was genuine that I had to respond. I'm not saying this to suck up to my bosses, nor did I say it then to curry favor from the producers, but to be the announcer for *The Price is Right*, in any medium, has always been a dream job for me. I have been aware of damn near every announcer of the television show since I was a kid. I used to mimic Johnny Olson's cadence, and tried to match his barrel-chested voice. I even learned copy from the show and commercials so I could practice rattling off facts about laundry detergent.

I sent off my resume, head shots, and cover letter, as-suming *The Price is Right LIVE!* posting on Craigslist was a hoax, and I didn't expect to hear another word about it. Much to my surprise, the ad was indeed the real deal, and a few days later I started my day with a phone call *and* an e-mail (clearly she's not from Vegas) from Cathy Dawson, the producer of *TPIRL*.

She had reviewed my resume and was hoping I would be interested in meeting with her to discuss the show's needs, my qualifications, and possibly, set up an audition. I was elated someone in Vegas had *finally* read my exten-sive resume and acted on my submission. I was even more excited by the opportunity being presented to me.

We set up a meeting where I would get to chat with Cathy and watch the show to get a feel for how things worked. Cathy Dawson is a wonderful woman and a true professional in the entertainment world. She has been working in television for many years, and her father-in-law was the legendary comedian, and host of *Family Feud*, Richard Dawson. I showed up well-dressed and early for our meeting. She thanked me for being early, citing how few entertainers in Las Vegas were able to make their ap-pointments. I felt more confident about the prospect of landing the job already. Knowing how shallow the talent pool in Las Vegas can be, this didn't exactly shock me. I happily offered to recommend a few people which took her by surprise. "Really? Why would you do that?" She asked. I told her, "These are people I have worked with in the past, and, if I can't have the job, I would much rather a good, qualified friend should have it." I truly believe this went a long way toward my ultimately getting the job.

Cathy asked me about my experience in entertainment, the credits on my resume, and was quite interested in my writing. She didn't give me the third degree or anything, but she certainly did her due diligence. We enjoyed a genuine conversation, which I think was also refreshing to her. After hearing some of the stories she told me about their recent talent search, I could only imagine how much she appreciated hearing intelligent things being said by someone who, at least on the surface, was not a typical Vegas flake.

I had a front row center seat in the beautiful Jubilee Theater for the show, and was told to pay particular attention to JD Roberto, who was announcing for Todd Newton that day. I was warned that JD tended to be a little faster paced with his audience warm-up than most, but she was more concerned I take in the full show and get an idea of what sort of thing I may be getting myself into. I loved learning that the announcer was the first person anyone saw on stage for this show, and that there was a stand-up comedy element to the presentation.

The show was truly exciting; I was thrilled to see the sets, the big dollar signs, the bright colors, and the famous

The Price is Right logo on the center door. I don't know why I got so giddy at seeing the logo. I laughed to myself and thought "What the hell did you think you were going to see, Martello?"

All the requisite things from a game show, particularly *TPIR*, were in place. I was as happy to see games like Hole in One, Cliffhangers, and Plinko as anyone else in that audience. I compared JD's performance to some of my favorite announcers, and thought about how I would do the job during my upcoming audition which we would schedule within a week or so after this viewing . . . *If* executive producers, Andy Felsher and Jeff Palmer, liked my resume and her notes about my interview.

Cathy suggested I visit the show once more to see a different host and announcer take the stage before my audition. This time the show featured Mark L. Walberg as the host and comedian/juggler Daniel Rosen as the announcer. Seeing another man with a background in comedy and juggling made me feel a little better about my prospects.

While the two shows offered the same games and excitement, the presentation was like night and day. Mark, while similar in style to Todd, had a completely different approach and demeanor as he held the long microphone. Rosen was more like a circus ringmaster than Roberto. I mean, he even wore a gaudy salmon-pink suit! I was reassured by Cathy that I wouldn't be required to wear a pink suit if I got the job. I was invited backstage to meet both of them and got a little more info from Cathy about the next steps.

When word came I would be auditioning, I had already worked out a warm-up routine. I wanted to make it my own, but stay true to what audiences were used to watching. Cathy sent me the link to a video of announcer Randy West performing the warm-up. I was instructed to use it as template for my own routine. The bullet points in West's warm-up were the same as the two times I saw the show live, but the presentation was a lot different, and only featured about half of the routine.

I had now seen three different people doing the routine, and I was more than ready for an audition. I went to the Jubilee Theater and ran through a bit of my presentation a couple of times for Cathy. She liked my stage presence and sense of humor, and gave me a few notes to go over and apply toward my audition with the producers.

A few days later, Cathy called to set up an audition with one of the executive producers, Andy Felsher. She asked if I had watched the Randy West video, and I assured her I had. When the time came for me to go onto the stage, I knew my jokes, the order of the routine, and how to play to the room as if the 900-seat showroom were full instead of their only being two people watching me.

Around this time, I remembered how much I hate auditions. Most seem to involve a waiting room full of people who look and sound exactly like you who hope you suck, while inside another room a group of production people — who have seen everything already and doubt you'll have anything to offer — are hungry as hell and just want to go to lunch.

Andy Felsher stopped me a few times to give me notes. He also commented on my stage presence and had a few questions before I was allowed to do my full presentation.

When I finished, I had expected to receive some sort of response. I didn't need applause or anything, but a blink of an eye, a cough, any sound or reaction whatsoever would have been nice. Instead, I received stunned silence and blank stares. I assumed I was horrible. Andy Felsher asked, "Where's the rest of it?" I asked him to clarify. "The other half of the warm-up. You only did about five minutes. Where is the other five? You *did* watch Randy's tape, right?"

Now it was making sense. The video I had been asked to watch and base my routine on was only about four minutes in length. I explained this, and mentioned that I had assumed they didn't want to watch a full ten-minute audition from however many people they were interviewing. Andy shot a laser beam of frustrated confusion to Cathy who asked me if I was sure I watched the whole video. I calmly pulled out my phone and found the link to show them.

"If you give me about a minute or two, I'll just do a full routine based upon the two performances I've watched," I said. "I remember most of it. I just need a moment to recall a few key points."

Cathy came up onstage and whispered, "Are you sure? That would really be great." I assured her I could do it, and she offered a couple of the main points for me to incorporate. After a couple minutes, I rattled off a full ten minutes of energetic *Price is Right* themed material. Cathy seemed happy with the performance, but Andy still seemed to be startled by the video issue. When I was done, he said, "It's clear you have stage presence and a good voice. I just need to think about this. We have other people to watch." I thanked them both for the opportunity, and assumed this would be the last time I would ever say the words "*Come on Down!*"

A few days passed, and I was called in to audition for executive producers, Andy Felsher and Jeff Palmer in a dressing room/office inside Bally's. Cathy told me in confidence that I was her first choice, but the decision was not hers to make. At this point, the candidate pool had been narrowed down to four people.

The experience in that dressing room was a lot like a classic good cop/bad cop interrogation scene in a movie. While I have always gotten along with both men, there couldn't be two more vastly different personalities. Jeff Palmer is possibly the happiest man on the planet, while Andy Felsher is more of a stern, down-to-business task-master. The two of them certainly could have made great characters in a buddy comedy.

This audition wasn't about the warm-up, I was asked to read copy. I always tell people I only got this job be-cause I could read and talk at the same time. I was about to prove it to the *TPIRL* cop buddies. I was given copy about various prizes and grocery items, and even a script from a past showcase so they could hear how well I did a cold read, how clearly I could be understood, and how quickly I could rattle off the many features of *A New Car!*

Jeff seemed to like some of my jokes and commented about a few of the little Johnny Olson-esque lilts and phrases I used. Andy had a lot of questions about my background and was very curious as to why I had so little television experience. I think I auditioned well, but I really had no idea where things were going.

In total, I ended up auditioning four times. At one point, I was asked to come in just moments *after* I had auditioned to watch the program again and then do a final onstage reading for Andy Felsher.

When my last words had been spoken and the countdown and introduction for the show had played, I was called down into the orchestra pit. Andy told me he was prepared to give me a two-week trial in the hopes things would work out. I was very happy to accept, and asked a few questions about when I would start, what I should wear, and what, if anything, I'd be getting paid for this trial. Andy looked at me and said, "Did you ask *if* you were getting paid? Do you really think *The Price is Right* wouldn't pay its talent?" What he didn't know was there are a *lot* of unscrupulous producers in Vegas who absolutely *loved* to take advantage of fresh-faced entertainers in such a way. It's show biz, and bad things happen. I smiled and said, "Well, I guess I don't think that anymore." We shook hands and I waited for further instructions from Cathy.

I came in after another show with Mark Walberg and Daniel Rosen to fill out paperwork, including a non-disclosure agreement and a rather lengthy document explaining it was a felony to cheat at a game show. It seems the quiz show scandals of the 50s and 60s had left a rather large mark on the game show world, and that paperwork went a long way toward scaring the hell out of anyone associated with game shows. Cathy reassured me the payroll paperwork meant I would be getting paid for my two week trial, and if I could be patient, a contract would be forthcoming. She also told me I was the only non-television, non-L.A. talent they had ever hired for the Vegas show. They had used others in their residency shows across the country, but for Vegas, they always wanted a Hollywood guy with lots of TV credentials. I was grateful they were willing to take a chance on me.

Two weeks turned into four. Four became eight. Eight became sixteen. Paychecks came in steadily. Every so often, I asked if I would ever be given a contract. "I kind of need to know if I have the job," I said with a laugh. Cathy said quietly, "If you wouldn't mind simply showing up every day until I can get confirmation from Andy, that would be lovely." I never did receive a contract or confirmation that I got the job, but I showed up every day and I loved every minute of it.

Presently, I am four years into my two-week trial as the announcer for *The Price is Right LIVE!*. As a result, I have traveled the U.S. and Canada several times on tour and entertained over one million people.

To the best of my knowledge, there are only five *TPIRL* hosts I have not worked with: Alan Thicke, Doug Davidson, Roger Lodge, Michael Burger, and George Hamilton. As a result of this show, and through my long history in live entertainment, my host count is at an astonishing eleven. Eleven of the most talented, diverse, and remarkable people I have worked with in my thirty years as a live performer, ten of whom I interviewed for this book. I have worked with Emmy-winners, bestselling authors, and platinum-selling musicians. I have learned a *lot*.

My motivation behind writing this book was to not only share what it is like to work with such extremely talented people, but to pick the brains of the masters, shed some light on what they believe makes a great host, and find out, specifically, what is it like not just to host a game show, but how to be an outstanding television presenter.

In my mind, hearing the tricks of the trade is invaluable to anyone interested in pursuing, or continuing, a career in entertainment. These men have hosted all types of programs, and many of the methods they utilize on television or on stage translate well into many other aspects of entertainment, if not virtually *any* job where leadership and dealing with the public are of paramount importance. Moreover, there are not many shows, onstage or on screen, which can boast almost universal recognition, long-standing history, and a long list of people who have hosted the program like *TPIRL!*.

What makes this list of people interesting to me is that these gentlemen have had to host this show while fighting the battle of not being Bob Barker or Drew Carey.

To be able to take the stage and host a beloved show people know by heart and make it their own without taking anything away from *The Price is Right* legacy is no easy feat.

I believe all of these men start their task of hosting *TPIRL* with an immediate disadvantage since so many in the audience expect Bob or Drew, even though the tickets and posters are very clear to explain this is a stage show hosted by [*insert name here*]. Yet, when the show is over, I am hard-pressed to find anyone who walks out of the theater and feels as though they didn't see (a few adaptations aside) *The Price is Right*. A unique group of people is represented in this book and on stages across North America playing to thousands of people every year. I know I have benefitted as a performer from my experiences working with them, and I am hopeful you will benefit reading the words from them. You don't have to be an entertainer to learn a lot about interacting with people from these professionals. I am grateful for their time, and for humoring me with this project.

Everyone I have worked with has been fun, professional, and friendly. I wish this were some sort of seedy tell-all full of tales of debauchery and mayhem to amuse and titillate you. I certainly *could* have written some of that sort of thing, but, admittedly, while not everything that has happened can (or should) be shared here, much of it is quite tame by most people's standards. The big thing to remember is, we're all professionals and, aside from the paycheck, we really are in this to have fun.

With that in mind, get ready, Television Fans! It's time for the hosts to *Come on Down!*

....

TWO

A CONVERSATION W TH
RICHARD LAWRENCE

Throughout this book, you will find a handful of names pop up more frequently than others. It seems there is quite a lot of interplay among game show personnel. Producers, interns, writers, onstage talent, and countless other staffers end up working with "everybody" sooner or later.

One name came up most often during my interviews, and that was Richard Lawrence. Why? Lawrence has represented or done business with several of the hosts I have worked with over the years, including Todd Newton, Mark L. Walberg, JD Roberto, Pat Finn, Dave Ruprecht, and Marc Summers. In fact, when it comes to game show hosts, he is the go-to guy — both as an agent and as a source for information. From Dick Clark to Wink Martindale, Johnny Gilbert to George Fenneman, Regis Philbin to Vanna White, he has worked with them all. He's the guy who brought the lovely Vanna to the set of *Wheel of*

Fortune and *Judge Judy* to the airwaves. If you are looking for a person with the knowledge and pedigree to speak authoritatively about what makes a great host, Richard Lawrence is on a very short list of people to call.

"My dad was a game show announcer in New York," said Lawrence. "He worked about 8 ½ years on a show called *The Big Payoff*. In those days they shot daily. Not like today where they tape five episodes a day. I would go in with him to work every day, and the time in the studio with him was the best. I said 'I want to do THIS.'"

After 2 ½ years of trying to make it in Buffalo as on-air talent at a few rock n' roll radio stations, he moved out to Los Angeles hoping to be one of the big voices in radio and television. However, he was not met with much luck. Possessing a keen eye for talent and how things worked in the business, he realized why he wasn't getting the bookings. "I wasn't as *good* as these guys."

Lawrence has always had an affinity for the classic broadcasters, citing their reliability and showmanship for their longevity as true professionals. "Up until recently, Wink Martindale was still on the air!" He was eventually hired at the Abrams-Rubaloff talent agency, who specialized in television hosts and announcers.

"I started handling voiceover talent first," said Lawrence. "Announcers are the unsung heroes of the business. They do what they do, and they do it well, and they don't get paid a hell of a lot either. That's why they do a lot of shows." Before long, he was representing hosts, which was a little nerve-racking at first. "Some of the clients I ended up bringing into the agency. Others were already there." One of his first big client visits was with Regis Philbin. "He was the announcer and sidekick for the Joey Bishop Show, and I was told I had to go 'service him'. I had no idea what that meant," he said with a laugh. He was told to go to the set and talk to Philbin, whom he met backstage in a dressing room. "I was so nervous," admitted Lawrence. Regis, a bit standoffish, asked, "Who are you?" Lawrence said he was from Abrams-Rubaloff, and Regis replied with a happy, "OH! You're my agent." After a few pleasantries, Philbin pulled Richard aside and posed a rather important question, "How come I'm not Ed McMahon?" Richard smirked and said, "I started [*with the agency*] three weeks ago. Give me another week and I'll have an answer for you." Clearly this guy had a quick wit and a knack for making his clients feel comfortable. "I always stand behind my clients, either figuratively or literally."

Having worked with so many of the greatest hosts in the business, Richard has a love for the art as well as a love for the people he's worked with. "My belief is being a game show host could be one of the most difficult jobs.

The job is to make it look easy and fun. They are incredible people. They make it fresh every show." According to Lawrence, "Some people can just walk in and do it. Dick Clark was one of those hosts who could do anything."

Lawrence speaks with great reverence about many of the personalities he has represented over the years, calling the aforementioned Clark "Such a wonderful man" and Peter Marshall "a true gentleman." He loves the business and craft of hosting, and realizes it's not a field just anyone can master. Having had such a long career in Hollywood bringing friendly faces to your television screens, I asked him what he saw in people that would make them excellent hosts. According to Lawrence, the most common denominator is a general affability. "99% of the people I've represented were nice guys. A few were difficult to work with. All the other guys were thrilled to go to work." When asked to provide other qualities which make for a fantastic host, he offered this: "Broadcasters are the best; people from radio or TV who grew up watching it." He went on to cite Todd Newton, who started as a radio DJ, as a wonderful example. "Todd is true to his roots and a great host."

He has noticed a wide variety of changes between when he started and today, including where new talent is found. "Hosting has changed a lot. In the old days, a lot of the guys had done several shows before, or were comedians. Peter Marshall was a lounge singer when he was signed on to do *Hollywood Squares*. In today's television market, most game show hosts are guys who have had sitcoms."

If not sitcom stars, more and more game show hosts seem to come from places not necessarily suited for a traditional game show. It's not uncommon to see a fashion consultant from Bravo or a chef from the Food Network hosting a game show or another type of competition. This is not lost on Lawrence. "The reason they hire people from other mediums is they think it is an easier sell [*to a network*]. When they put Guy Fieri in as the host of a game show, they are thinking, 'If he did well on *Diners, Drive-ins, and Dives*, he'll do well on *Minute to Win it*.' Success brings success."

The biggest change he sees is in the lack of opportunities for hosts to find work. "The hardest part of my job is when my clients are not working," said the agent. "When I started, there were 17 daytime network game shows. Now there are two: *The Price is Right* and *Let's Make a Deal*." He is all too correct. While there are several more networks, there are precious few hosting gigs. Even with the syndicated editions of shows like *Family Feud*, *Wheel of Fortune*, *Jeopardy!*, and *Who Wants to Be a Millionaire*, there are not as many chances for a qualified host to find a good job. In addition, as with all good things on television, there are not many guarantees. "Every show that goes on the air except *Wheel*, *Jeopardy*, the late night talk shows, and the news get cancelled," he said with a smirk. An argument could be made to include *The Price is Right* on that list.

Knowing that hosting jobs are considerably less prevalent than 40 years ago, I asked who in the modern days of hosting (game shows or otherwise) did he see as top-of-their-game talent, and where new talent is found. "David Letterman was wonderful. I like Jimmy Kimmel too," he said. "It seems a lot of the new hosts are coming from YouTube. Have you seen Chris Hardwick on *@Midnight*? He is fantastic. [*Mimicking Hardwick*] 'POINTS!' He is a great example of one of the new kinds of hosts."

Having already offered his opinion of Todd Newton, I asked Richard to share a few thoughts on some of the other people that he and I have both worked with. After all, every single person I spoke to about him had nothing but good things to say, which is rare in Hollywood. Really now . . . talent *not* complaining about their agent?

"I'll speak highly of them! They are all such great guys to work with," said Lawrence.

On Dave Ruprecht: "I met Dave Ruprecht because I was representing Mark Walberg at the time on *Shop 'til You Drop* [*Mark was the announcer*]. The producer of that show also did *Supermarket Sweep* [*with Ruprecht*] and I went on the set to meet with Mark and the producer and saw Dave. Ruprecht did such a fine job with that show."

On Mark L. Walberg: "Mark Walberg can do anything. He can walk into a situation the night before a show is going to tape and do it as if he had rehearsed for weeks. A natural host, very likable, and a good family guy"

On Pat Finn: "Pat is somebody I feel very comfortable with. When Pat came here to see us, I told him this is going to take a year [*before he got work*]. I sent him in for an audition. CAA [*Creative Artists Agency*] called and said, 'We really like this guy, but can't make a decision. Why don't we give him $1500 in good faith to put him on hold?' I told Pat he just made money for auditioning. They did this to him two or three times. By the time they made a decision it was a week later and everyone in town thought people were lining up to get him. It took much less than a year. He is amazing."

On Bob Goen: "Bob has been with me since 1984. I still have the humidor he gave me after he got *Entertainment Tonight*. There were a lot of celebrities on that show [ET] who requested to be interviewed by him. Truly one of the greatest employees *ever* to a company."

Lawrence also had a hand in introducing Goen to his future wife, comedienne and actress, Marianne Curan. "Marianne came into my office and said, 'You know who

I'd like to meet? Bob Goen.' Bob had just broken up with his first wife and I told her there's a line around the block to meet Bob. I told her I would send him her tape, her photograph, and her bio, but please don't bug me about this! I sent them over and 2 ½ weeks later he calls me, asking, 'Should I meet her?'."

On JD Roberto: "For such a young guy, he was a natural."

On Marc Summers: "Marc worked with us for 28 years. He was here when I bought the company. I made the first *Double Dare* deal for him and deals for many of his shows. He is not with us now, but he still calls to get my opinion on things. To me, he's part of the family.

Richard Lawrence has seen the hey-day of television game shows and presenters, and the transition into the modern era. He works tirelessly for his clients and has a stellar reputation for finding good on-air homes for talented people. As my interview with him at his company, Rebel Entertainment Partners, Incorporated, came to a close, I asked him if he had any parting thoughts.

"It's funny. I hated being an agent for the first few years. Today, I feel privileged to have worked with these guys."

THREE

....

MARK L. WALBERG

"To be a great host I think you have to be selfless to some degree. You have to be the facilitator of the episode of television, not the gatherer of attention to you. In a game show, you have to be an expert in running the game fairly and efficiently. That comes easy for me."

- Mark L. Walberg

....

From the first day I worked with him, I've had to clarify that I'm referring to the long-time host Mark Walberg and not the film actor. I like to do this is by pointing out some of the recognizable shows he has hosted, and by explaining that he is the *first* famous Mark Walberg. One of our mutual friends refers to him as "The Markier Mark." Watching him on television, I always assumed he was a man with a quick wit and good sense of humor. My assumptions were proven correct after seeing him perform live onstage.

Being something of a television junkie and a lover of game shows, I was already familiar with Mark's work. I remember him as the host of *Russian Roulette*, and FOX's *Temptation Island* (one of my guilty pleasures). *Temptation Island* was a rather tawdry and difficult show to host, and to do it without appearing at all seedy or lecherous speaks well of his abilities and his affable nature. By the time I met him, he was working steadily as the host of another of my favorite shows, *Antiques Roadshow* on PBS.

We met briefly after a show I watched him host, and he was very friendly and encouraging. By the time I was onstage working with him, he made sure I felt comfortable. He'd performed audience warm-up several times in his early career on television, so he knew the job.

Having watched Mark onstage before, I knew about what to expect, but a show is completely different when you are on stage instead of in the audience. I knew I would have a lot more to watch no matter who was hosting. Aside from constantly having to check my list of names and prize copy, watching for specific cues within the show, staging mishaps, and other things that only happen in live theater, I always had to pay attention to the host. At any point, there could be an opportunity for interaction in that classic Johnny Carson/Ed McMahon way, and I would need to be ready.

Mark has a boyish charm and soothing presence that puts the nervous and shaking contestants at ease. Maybe this is due to his blue eyes or the fact that many watch him on *Antiques Roadshow*, a decidedly calmer program — until someone learns their attic crap is worth college tuition, that is. "It's pretty simple, actually," he explained. "For me, the contestant is everything. I try to project my interest/affection for them instantly. You can feel them let go and relax. I always keep a hand on their back or arm or something. It sounds creepy, but touching them —appropriately! — lets them know they're taken care of. But, really it starts from the moment you come on stage. Are you [*the host*] projecting 'I'm a big star. Don't mess with me' or 'I'm just like you and I can't wait to meet you!'?"

One thing I noticed in particular about his approach to hosting the show is his very brisk pace. The show moved quickly, but there was never any sort of feeling anything was being rushed. Contestants got their moment to shine, enjoyed the classic game show interview, and were expertly informed on the rules of play. This faster pace maintained the already frenzied feeling in the theater, and energy was very high. According to Mark, "Every time I do the show, I learn something more. JD Roberto also works at lightning pace. He's very good, by the way. I tried picking up the pace just for fun and found that the show went so much better."

Mark is excellent at making sure I am a part of any show we work, well beyond names and prizes. "I feel very comfortable 'playing' with you. I know you're a pro and will only take me to a good place. But, in general, I'm confident sharing that time," Mark said. "By involving the announcer and models, you give yourself the chance of something great happening organically." He doesn't provide a lot of banter back and forth, but I believe the overall pacing of the show with him at the helm doesn't allow for too many of those moments. Unnecessary chatter would just slow things down in an awkward way. However, when those moments do arise, they are always well-placed or otherwise necessary. "Most announcers are pros. They are good. It would be stupid not to 'cherry pick' off their performance abilities and experience. It's different with every announcer."

I also enjoy working with Mark because he has always been very supportive of my work. I found out long after I had the job with *TPIRL* that he was rather vocal to the executive producers about how well he thought I fit in. Believe me, there were times when I was almost certain I really didn't have the job, even though I was collecting a paycheck for it, and Mark went to bat for me whenever he could.

Prior to our series of shows in Indio, CA near Palm Springs, Mark had worked on a different show produced by the same people. The announcer for that show could best be described as *not* your prototypical ideal game show announcer. He didn't have an *announcer voice* or a background in reading copy. By the time Mark and I met up in Indio, I had heard more than my share of stories about this announcer's presentation.

As rehearsal got underway, I was going through my prize copy, reading my script into the mic. Much to my surprise, Mark quite suddenly stopped the rehearsal. In front of our producer, Mark exclaimed loudly, "May I just say how refreshing it is to be working with a *professional* again? Thank *God*, you're here, Andy!" It was both embarrassing and touching. I know it seems strange, but those little, unnecessary gestures, really made me feel as though I was more than just a guy who happened to be available for the show dates.

Truly generous and encouraging people in entertainment are extremely rare. Most people live the dog-eat-dog existence, but Mark is usually the first to recommend good people for good work. "Being able to do a live show is significantly different than a taped one. The people I've recommended are all pros in that area." There isn't an unlimited supply of work in show business, and for a host to lead the producers to another well-qualified host is a sign of a professional and a good man.

Mark even contributed to the fundraising project for my first book, and offered a great testimonial for the back cover. I will be forever grateful for his support and friendship. I could not have asked for a better man to welcome me into the game show world.

....

Mark L. Walberg on:

- **Being a great Host**

The key is to be authentic, no matter what the subject matter. That doesn't mean being the *same* every time. I'm authentic, but different when I hang with my pals [*compared to*] when I'm talking to my kids. The most important tool is to be in the moment. Don't plan your jokes or comebacks. Listen. In the talk/reality world, silence is a huge tool. If you sit silently, your guest will have to fill the space with words. It's in those moments when things get revealed that take the show off the page. I just try to project to the audience that I have this thing under control and we're all going to have a blast together.

- **Strengths and Weaknesses**

I'm not a huge presence like Todd Newton. I may be less animated than some. I like to think I'm good at being in the moment. I'd say connecting with the contestants onstage and with the audience, in an authentic way, might be a strength. I'm pretty good at running the games.

- **The Contestants**

For me, the contestant is everything. I approach game shows as I approach most things. I try to make an early connection with the audience. I also try to let the contestants be the star. I'm not looking to steal the thunder. I'm the host. The show is the draw here. Then, you have to *choose* to be interested in everyone that comes on stage. Have fun with the contestant. Make sure they're making you laugh and the audience will come along. On *Roadshow*, it's very much the same, but not about fun and laughter. It's about education and fascination. I *choose* to be interested in everything we discuss. That interest translates to the home audience.

• Nervous Contestants

I'm a co-dependent kind of guy! [*laughing*] But, I try to talk to them, not around them. I listen closely. I try and project that I'm their friend and they're safe with me. If you're in the zone, you can sense just how far you can go with the people.

• Drunk Contestants

Never give up the mic! [*laughing*] You must always project control over your domain. Even the most obnoxious, drunk person doesn't want to be embarrassed. The host has the advantage of power. Never give up the advantage and never be heavy handed. If you back a snake in a corner, it will strike. If you give them a graceful exit, no one gets hurt.

- **Not being Bob Barker or Drew Carey**

I run into this thing all the time. I have a bit of an advantage in that I've been on air for a couple decades, so there's some recognition. But, it comes back to connecting with the audience. I'll give props to Drew and Bob, but in 30 seconds the audience decides if they're with you or not. I try to project fun, love, and confidence. I feel that about a minute into the experience, the audience is over the Bob/Drew thing!

- **Favorite Moments**

I remember sending a lady up a set stairs to play a game where she could win $5,000. As she ascended the stairs, she slipped and almost fell off the platform. I said she almost won $500,000.

- **Idols and Influences**

Dick Clark was amazing. He could stretch to fill time and add content while he did it. He was authentic and audiences connected. He taught me that, when on camera, you're talking to one person not millions.

In the talk show world, it's [Johnny] Carson. He taught me to let the guest score. It projects on you as the host like you're the star. You see, if you go for every joke, even if they hit, you're saying "Don't you think I'm funny?" But, if you allow your guest to have the punch line and very conservatively pick your moments, you're now saying, "I know I'm funny. Or smart. Or engaged." and the audience senses that.

....

Mark L. Walberg has been the host of the Emmy-nominated Antiques Roadshow, the longest running prime time PBS television series and presently produces and hosts Buried History on PBS.

....

FOUR

BOB GOEN

"The contestants *must* know that they have a friend, an advocate, with them on stage. Otherwise, the fear and nerves can paralyze them, and that's the worst thing that can happen."

- Bob Goen

....

B ob Goen may have been the host I most looked forward to meeting. Growing up as a game show fan, I recall seeing Bob on my TV screen often. He was my favorite anchor on *Entertainment Tonight*, and I always enjoyed his interviews. I remember when he took over as the host of *Wheel of Fortune*, and I remember when he rocked a classic, late-70s moustache. For me, Bob Goen was the last of that great tradition of classic game show hosts during the final hey-day of game shows as a staple on daytime television. When I heard that I was getting the chance to work with Bob, I felt like I had somehow made it, and he made me feel like I was in the right place; that I not only belonged on stage with him, but deserved the job. He offered great advice on presentation, tone, and inflection. Backstage, he would present my microphone to me as if handing a warrior his weapon of choice. His baritone voice would bring me on stage with an introduction that demanded applause from the audience. He shared stories and coached me. Bob seemed just as fascinated with my career in comedy and as a juggler as I was in his game show pedigree. He's also a cigar smoker, so we got along very well from the start.

I have joked with Bob many times about how I thought he was on the Mount Rushmore of *Entertainment Tonight* hosts, sitting pretty with Mary Hart, John Tesh, and Leeza Gibbons. Meeting him in person, I thought he missed his calling. His presence matched that of Powers Boothe, and his stature certainly would have made him a great western hero.

Very much a traditional game show host, he offers humor and wit when and where it's necessary to put the contestants at ease. He isn't a fast-paced, fast-talking host, but he is one of the best. He is direct, and makes certain the rules are both thoroughly explained and well understood. I think his people skills are among the things that set him apart.

Choosing contestants at random certainly makes for a better experience from a "Will I get picked?" standpoint, but from a "Will this make for an entertaining show?" point of view, it isn't always ideal. "We've had contestants who absolutely froze. There's nothing you can do about that. It's random," said Bob. "All you can do is try to be as entertaining as possible." Bob makes sure every contestant gets their moment on stage. He interviews the contestants the same way he would any Hollywood celebrity, and I think he is well-liked by the audience for that reason. His ability to draw out the interesting nuggets from people who don't feel they live exciting lives is a trait not many in the business possess.

He has a wry sense of humor, peppering in little quips with a slow-forming, endearing smile. He introduces the game Plinko, as "Plin Co", and has even created a back story about the fictitious company and their many miracle products. He uses his TV voice to act out mock commercials. "From the fine folks at Plin Co., comes the handy kitchen gadget no home can live without . . "

Bob makes certain the announcer is very much a person in the show and not just a voice from the stage. When he has to do something with a prop on stage requiring a bit of dexterity, he looks toward me says, "Andy, you should be doing this. You're the magician on this stage!" This would frequently lead into a brief discussion about my entertainment resume. He would often plug my website and tout my skills as an entertainer, actor, and even as a writer (even though I don't believe he's ever read a darned thing I've written). I was always humbled by the praise. "You are so good, you're so quick, and so glib. It brings another layer to the presentation that builds and makes it a better product by the end," he would tell me. It's easy to feel liked and supported when someone steps away from the limelight to offer a little of it to the unknown guy on the stage.

I always felt he allowed just the right amount of interaction with the announcer. "You're an integral part of the show. The audience needs to know you as much as they know me, and they don't get to know you if you're just reading copy," said Bob. "When I first started working shows with my good friend David Ruprecht, who was announcing for me, the interaction on stage was an easy habit to get into when you have a dear friend sharing the stage with you. When you came along, I wanted that same dynamic, that same rapport."

Bob is the only host who has been to my home for a meal. In 2012, we found ourselves booked in Las Vegas over the Thanksgiving holiday. Every year, I offer an invitation to my entertainer friends who may not have family nearby, or have to work during the holiday. That particular Thanksgiving remains among my favorites. To hear some of the stories Bob shared from interviewing the likes of Milton Berle, the stories that certainly couldn't make it to the airwaves (and won't be repeated here), all while enjoying a beer, smoking a cigar, and watching old episodes of *The Muppet Show*, is one for the record books. Plus, there was just something oddly memorable about eating a Thanksgiving meal and hearing the booming voice of Bob Goen asking for seconds. For the record, in that same voice, he has described my turkey dinner as "a sumptuous repast". Maybe I should mention that to Marc Summers with the hope that he would get me on the Food Network.

Most recently, Bob found yet another way to make this newbie feel like the voice of choice. I was set to play several shows in Cincinnati in February of 2014 with host, Jerry Springer. Bob and his lovely wife, Marianne Curan, host a popular morning radio program in that area, and they were running some promos for the show, giving away tickets to contest winners and callers. The contest was a basic pricing game. In this case, two callers were asked to listen to some prize copy about an item and guess the price. The contestant closer to the price without going over won tickets to our show. He sent me a text message asking if I would be able to record about five spots for the show, which I was more than happy to do.

He sent me the prize copy and I prepared to rattle off some classic game show crooning into a microphone when I received another message from Bob. 'In the interest of full disclosure, Andy, I should let you know I did ask one other person to do this for me, but I don't think he'll be able to do it." I found this amusing for him to even worry about telling me this. It was just a freebie favor, so it really didn't matter. Then I read the other name on this very short list of candidates. It was legendary announcer and host, Johnny Gilbert.

Johnny, among many other things was the second announcer for the original *The Price is Right* (the Bill Cullen-hosted version), replacing the great Don Pardo. He is also the long-time announcer for another iconic game show, *Jeopardy!*.

I immediately told him there would be no love lost if I lost out to the legend. I also thanked him profusely. He thought I was thanking him for the heads-up about being his second choice, which was not the case. "Bob, thanks for putting me in such incredible company," I said. "I am damn near certain this will be the only time in my career my name will be in the same sentence as Johnny Gilbert's. I *know* it will be the only time we'd be in the same pay grade!" As it happened, my voice was the one used all week on their show, and he was very kind to speak so well of me on-air. He and Marianne even came to the show to do a pre-show segment, introducing me with style, kudos, and that booming baritone voice. I took some time out of my warm-up to stress to the crowd just what Bob's friendship and encouragement has meant to me over the years. He is a class act all the way.

....

Bob Goen On:

- ### Being a Great Host

The man who discovered me, Ray Horl, taught me this approach: As a game show host, you're hosting a dinner party. Everybody is sitting around your table. It is your job to make them feel comfortable. It's your responsibility to make sure they have a good time. If they have a good time, then your job is done.

- ### Strengths and Weaknesses

I always felt my strength in game shows was my focus on making the contestant feel comfortable, and their experience memorable. Their moment on stage will most certainly be one of the biggest memories of that person's life, and how dare I do anything to make that memory anything less than perfect. I can't guarantee that they will win anything, but I can ensure that they will have fun trying.

I guess the other thing I'm strong with was something that I had never considered, but it was said by Andy Felsher when he introduced Jerry Springer to me as the next host coming in. Andy said to Jerry, "This is Bob Goen, and he is the master of format." I honestly had never thought of myself that way, because I always have those little question marks in the back of my head that wonder if I'm missing something. I do know one thing though, I always try to be totally prepared when I walk out on stage. I run the show over and over and over in my living room before I go to the studio, and again and again and again in my dressing room before going on stage. It's just like you practicing a juggling or magic trick. You just can't afford to not be ready when you hit the stage. My biggest fear is that I'll be the guy who holds up a production because he didn't know his role. The greatest compliment you can give me is to call me "One Take" Goen!

As for my shortcomings, I guess that would have to be evaluated by producers I've worked with. After doing game shows for 30 years, you build up a real confidence about the work you do on stage. Otherwise, you can't deliver. But, I guarantee you there are people I've worked for who have been in the control room muttering, "Damn, if he would only . . ."

- **The Contestants**

Make the contestant shine, because they are the star of the show. I'm on your side. I want you to be your best. It's all about comfort level and disarming people so they are relaxed. [*Much like interviewing celebrities*] If you can get a conversation going, then you're fine.

- **The Nervous Contestants**

As the host of game shows, including when I hosted *Wheel of Fortune*, I would tickle the contestants. I'd give them noogies! Whatever it would take to relax them.

- **The Drunk Contestants**

[*laughing*] Give 'em *noogies!*

- **Not Being Bob Barker or Drew Carey**

On *Wheel of Fortune*, it was easy. I had a little thirteen-week buffer. When Pat Sajak left, he was replaced by a guy named Rolf Benirschke — a place kicker for the San Diego Chargers — who had never done television before. He didn't even know the red light on the camera meant the camera was on and he really struggled. By the time I got there, they [*audience and crew alike*] were ready for anybody who knew anything about the rudimentary things in TV.

I [*also*] had Vanna White there, and that makes a big difference. As long as Vanna is on the show, there's the credibility and she implies there's stamp of approval for me.

There's a basic template to doing every game show. You're following that template. In between the rules and the results, there's that little portion where you can be yourself. Drew Carey does it completely different from Bob Barker. He injects a completely different personality. That's what happens with us eleven hosts that you have worked with. You're the *only* person who knows the differences we all bring, which I find fascinating!

- **Favorite Moments**

There have been many. One that stands out, I remember doing a golf game in Branson, Missouri and I asked the contestant what he did for a living. He replied, "I'm a golf pro!" He was a teaching golf pro at a course in Branson! [*laughing*]

- **Idols and Influences**

I always looked up to game show hosts like Tom Kennedy, Geoff Edwards, and Bill Cullen. They were so relaxed, and seemed to be having such a good time. That's why I got into game shows. Everybody was just having *fun*. Including the hosts. What a way to make a living!

But the man I always tried to emulate — and fell woefully short of — was Dodgers broadcaster, Vin Scully. His games are poetic in their rhythm. He can call a baseball game and include a reference to Shakespeare, politics, and fine wine, all in the same inning. And yet, he never talks down to anyone. His class, elegance, humility, accessibility, dependability, knowledge, and preparation have always set him high above the crowd. My childhood was filled with summer evenings and his voice. I can't tell you how many nights I fell asleep with the transistor radio under my pillow, and Vinny's voice in my ear.

When I made it to *ET*, I sent him a letter to thank him for setting the bar for me, for giving me the template of quality that I've tried to live up to, and for all those summer nights. I just had to let him know the impact he had on me, both personally and professionally. Less than a week later in the mail, I received a hand written note of gratitude from Vinny that is still framed and hanging on my wall. Classy, elegant . . . perfect. I don't know why I would have expected anything less.

....

Bob Goen and his lovely wife Marianne Curan host the popular Bob & Marianne in the Morning Radio Show on WARM 98 in Cincinnati, Ohio five days a week.

FIVE

JOEY FATONE

"*The Price is Right* is a great all-American game show that's been around for many years, so, you want to keep that tradition [*as a host*]. When you do a live game show, anything goes."

- Joey Fatone

....

I firmly believe Las Vegas stays open an extra hour a day when Joey Fatone is in town. If anyone in the world has more fun than Joey, I would like to meet that person. Better yet, I'd like to introduce that person to him, alert the proper authorities, and capture the ensuing madness on video. Of course, the likelihood that he doesn't already know that person is pretty low.

Joey is very much the kid from the neighborhood; he is well liked by everyone, and appears to know *everyone*. He has stories about most of the celebrities you'd ever want to meet, and seems to remember the name of almost every person he has ever met. He will greet you with a big smile, a hug, and a very Italian "Aaayyyyy!" He is often recognized when he is out, and I have *never* seen him pass up the opportunity to make time to talk to a fan, pose for a photo, or sign an autograph.

What is remarkable about him is that with all the fame 'N Sync brought him, he is still able to blend seamlessly into a quiet restaurant and enjoy a meal. Of the higher profile celebrity hosts I have worked with, only he and Jerry Springer seem to have this ability.

He can be as foul-mouthed as a sailor on shore leave or as eloquent, polite, and charming as Miss Manners in the blink of an eye. Some of the funniest stories, dirtiest jokes, and best times I have had come from being around Joey Fatone.

How he manages to find the time to have so much fun is well beyond me. Work hard, play harder — and he's *always* working. You can't turn on the TV without seeing him hosting a new show or starring in a commercial. Whether he is striving for the coveted mirror ball trophy on *Dancing with the Stars*, taking the Broadway stage in *Rent*, or being eaten by a shark in *Jersey Shore Shark Attack*, he is one extremely busy man.

I could have mentioned *My Big Fat Greek Wedding* instead of *Jersey Shore Shark Attack*, but Joey is a real ballbuster who loves to crack wise. I'm sure he deserves a little comeback. I remember when my brother, Matt, came to Vegas once on vacation, and he wanted to see Joey and me working together . . . well, most likely he wanted to see Fatone. My brother has seen me on stage too many damn times. Within seconds of meeting Matt, Joey was joking around with him as if *he* were the brother and I was the smelly kid in grade school. "Man, Andy really sucked out there today, right?" Like I said, he is very much that kid from the neighborhood.

It's a party when Joey is hosting the show. The crew gets excited to have him around, the models prepare for the crazy conversations and the nights out on the town, and the fans show up in large numbers just to hear him make a few jokes about his former bandmates.

There is a genuine sense of fun when he is on stage. While he is a true host in many of the traditional ways, he tends to host with a game show meets frat party style. Well, an ABC Family version of a frat party.

He dances on stage, he beat-boxes during game music, and mimics a club DJ behind a prop game table. It is quite refreshing. There is definitely a youthful approach to how he hosts the show compared to many of the others. He manages to carry the tradition and history of classic game shows into a more modern era. Neither the rules nor the games are compromised, nothing is lost in the translation, and everyone is thoroughly entertained.

He is one who likes to banter with the announcer, and he definitely has no problem sharing the stage or funny lines that add to the moment. "I think the banter is a lot of fun. It brings the announcer more into the show. The announcer is kind of the person that moves the show along with the host. Like a sidekick for a superhero," says Fatone, a *huge* Superman fan.

I think the thing I enjoy most about working with him is how he includes everyone in his world, and how much he wants to be in yours. If he had some kind of special V.I.P. invitation to a club or an event while he was in town, he would make certain we were invited. When one of our ushers at the Jubilee Theater was having a party in town and extended the invitation to everyone at the show, Joey was there. Not just to make an appearance, but because he really wants to be everyone's friend.

Among my favorite, and longest, evenings with Joey involved a dirty metal band, plenty of alcohol, and a merging of two game show hosts.

Steel Panther is a, incredibly talented, wildly funny, and exquisitely raunchy heavy metal hair band act. They tour internationally and deliver one of the best shows any rock fan would love. Joey is a huge fan, and, whenever possible, he gets on stage with them to sing one of their most popular ballads. A quick search on YouTube will provide you with plenty of proof and entertainment in case you're curious. Steel Panther was playing at the House of Blues, and Joey had arranged for a booth to see them. One of our models, Amanda, and I were invited to join the fun. The show was tremendous, as always. Since I am not accustomed to bottle service and V.I.P. treatment, it was a fun way to enjoy an evening.

During the show, we learned that Drew Carey was in the audience. He was in Vegas with his Improv All-Stars show, and is also a big Steel Panther fan. Soon after Joey finished his rendition of Panther's *Community Property*, the lead singer did a little plug for *TPIRL*, and pointed out that Drew Carey was also in the crowd. "How screwed up is that? There are *two* game show hosts in here tonight?"

After the show we all headed backstage to hang with the band and enjoy the party. It was a ridiculous affair, and every bit of fun as you'd imagine. We all met Drew and enjoyed the food, beverages, and excitement backstage. Rikki Rockett from Poison was also there, along with the rest of Drew's All-Stars. When it was time to move the party elsewhere, Drew suggested we head out to the Ellis Island Casino to sing karaoke.

Ellis Island is a great casino for Vegas locals that offers excellent micro-brewed beer, good food, and karaoke every night. When Drew and his team walked in, he marched up to the karaoke KJ, tipped big, and made certain everyone got to sing. There was a large section of tables secured for us and drinks were on Mr. Carey, whom I never got to thank (*Thanks, Drew!*). Joey was a hit singing Rick Springfield's *Jesse's Girl*, and everyone in the bar got a kick out of singing karaoke with the likes of Drew and Joey. I can honestly say that my only encounter with Drew Carey was fantastic and he was extremely generous and kind to everyone he met that night. I know the wait staff was taken care of quite well, and if any of the locals complained about not getting stage time, they were more than happy to enjoy some drinks or food on Drew. It was a ton of fun.

It was also a night that probably didn't end until the sun was starting to come up. We *all* had to be back at work by 1 PM, so we certainly had some time to sleep, but I doubt much sleep happened. I am certain Joey still enjoyed time with friends after I dropped him off.

Aside from when I'm on tour, Joey is probably the host I have hung out with the most socially. There have been lunches, dinners, shows, and more karaoke than you can imagine. Somewhere, there's even a video of the two of us singing "Mustang Sally", but I'm certain it's not on YouTube. When he came back to town with *Dancing with the Stars LIVE*, he was more than happy to arrange tickets for me and my friends, and, as always, he had plenty of time for us. He always returns calls, texts, and emails, and when I see some of his new projects I try to bust his stones a bit. I enjoy the professional relationship as much as the personal one. Onstage, he is a charismatic host who brings his best every time he treads the boards. Offstage, he is a great friend. Above all else, he is a fun guy.

....

Joey Fatone on:

- **Being a Great Host**

Have fun with it. That's the main important thing and to hopefully get the people to have fun. [*From the other hosts*] I learned to take my time. Be able to be on the same level with the contestant or the person you're interviewing. You don't want to seem awkward or to make people nervous. The constant repetition helped me brush up on my hosting skills. Practice, practice, practice!

- **Strengths and Weaknesses**

My [*biggest*] strength is I make people feel comfortable on stage kind of kind a like the guy next-door.

[*My weakness is*] I always want to rush things and I tend to mumble my words.

- **The Contestants**

You never know what you're going to get from a contestant. Expect the unexpected. You want them to win.

You don't want to see them lose. Basically, you are rooting for them and being on their side.

- **The Nervous Contestants**

It all depends on how the person is. A host is good at learning their body language, which I pick up right away — Whether they want to be touched as far as putting your arm around them, holding their hand, giving them a very calm voice or excited voice.

- **The Drunk Contestants**

I had a guy who kept screaming out different boy band names. I told him to shut the hell up and the crowd went crazy. They loved it. Then, he proceeded to keep going. So, I told him he must like guys and I'll get him Lance Bass' number! The crowd went crazy [*laughing*].

- **Not Being Bob Barker or Drew Carey**

Every show, I just came out and explained who I was, if they didn't know, and I let them know it's a live show. Not a TV show [*laughing*]. There were no nerves. Only if I screwed up the game by accident or said a different price.

- **Favorite Moments**

There's always the fun drunk people on stage. Either they curse, yell, and get upset or they go crazy when they win.

- **Idols and Influences**

Bob Barker, Wink Martindale, Chuck Woolery, and one of the great ones, Johnny Carson. Also, Tom Bergeron.

....

Joey Fatone is the host of The Live Well Network's My Family recipe Rocks! He is also the announcer for Family Feud with Steve Harvey and owner of his own restaurant, Fat One's Hot Dogs.

SIX

....

TODD NEWTON

....

"Hosting is not a hobby or a plan B. It is my art and my craft. It is what I have wanted to be and do since I first saw Johnny Carson in 1982."

- Todd Newton

....

H e is America's Alpha Male. He is a larger than life personality and a supreme live performer. He has a commanding presence on stage like no one else I've worked with, and he oozes confidence in every way. He has a rapier wit and comedic timing that rival the world's best comedians. An Emmy-winner equally at home with Hollywood's biggest celebrities as he is with Mildred from Indiana, he has the ability to make everyone around him feel comfortable. He is the Host with the Most — He even owns the trademark. He is TODD NEWTON!

It's difficult for me to put into words what it's like working with Todd Newton, especially when he is right in front of me. No really, he is in the seat directly in front of me as I write this while traveling to Toronto, Canada. We have toured the world, enjoyed countless beers, laughed thousands of times, chased after the same girls, ridden on tiny tour buses, flown on planes with Lynyrd Skynyrd —Hell, I'm the witness to his damned will for Heaven's sake! I have a feeling that if he knew I was working on his chapter right now, he would be moving his seat forward and back just to mess with me. We have worked hundreds of shows together and become very good friends.

Todd was the first person I ever watched host *TPIRL*, but it was quite some time before I got to work with him. I met Todd when we performed two special shows for the state lotteries. Sometime after that, he was back for a single week's worth of shows where I was the announcer. Before I started touring with him, Todd and I had worked together a total of seven times, and knew nothing about each other. Well, I knew about him, but he had no reason to know anything about me; I was the new guy and not at all famous.

I had seen Todd as the host of *Whammy! The All New Press Your Luck*, *Hollywood Showdown*, *Instant Millionaire*, and as a red carpet commentator on the E! television network. In fact, it was his appearances on E! that inspired one of my favorite Jimmy Fallon impersonations on *Saturday Night Live*. Look it up online, it's pretty damned funny.

Todd represents what I call the New Age of game show hosts. No longer daytime staples and pre-soap opera entertainment, game shows are either syndicated creations appearing at odd times and in different markets, or exist as evening pre-prime time favorites. Todd has popped up as the host of many of them.

Todd is very much the silverback of the *TPIRL* hosts, and has been there from day one, show one. When *TPIRL* took the stage at Harrah's Casino in Reno, Nevada, Todd was the host who walked through the center door. "It was 2002, I believe. I was shopping for a birthday present for my wife at the time," recalled Todd. "I received a phone call from Fremantle Media asking if I'd be interested in hosting the live theater version in Reno. My son had just been born and I was in between tapings of *Whammy!*, so I thought it would be a wonderful way to pick up a few bucks and have a little fun."

Todd turned out to be a great fit for the show and the show turned out to be a great fit for theaters and casinos. What started as a two-week trial for *TPIRL* in Reno turned into another two weeks, then a month, then a few months. Soon, it was being shopped around Atlantic City, Las Vegas, and elsewhere, and Todd Newton was the host audiences saw the most. People liked the idea of not traveling to Hollywood to see their favorite show, and they loved seeing Todd as the host. "I've been compared to Bob in his younger years but take it only as a compliment."

After Bob Barker announced his retirement, and as a result of these frequent appearances with the live show, conventional wisdom seemed to support Todd being on the very short list to take over. Actor George Hamilton was the front-runner of that list. According to Todd, "I knew that I was somewhat the underdog in the race. Everyone else that was being looked at had considerable celebrity status. Rather than being discouraged by that, I was actually fueled by it. I knew that people would be looking at me for what I could bring to the table rather than simply for what my name was. It was exciting."

Hearing this didn't surprise me at all. Todd takes on every challenge as an opportunity. He may appear confident and cocky to those who don't know him, but he is very much a humble man who happens to have a great sense of self-awareness. He knows exactly where he fits in the entertainment world and has always known his strengths and weaknesses along the way. He realizes when he's outgunned and he still goes into the fight.

George Hamilton had all the makings of a perfect replacement for Barker, were it possible to replace him. It seemed that the network was trying looking for a close carbon copy of Barker. Hamilton had the tan, the style, the suits, the hair, the charm, and the name. What he did not have was experience as a game show host, and the humility that comes with being an underdog.

While Fremantle was grooming Hamilton and testing the waters, Todd was preparing for his screen tests at CBS. He was scheduled to host two shows, and the network would be monitoring his performance and the audience reactions. "The truth is, I knew it was the biggest opportunity of my career," said Todd. He also knew most of the people patiently waiting in line were hoping to see Bob Barker. "I anticipated they might be disappointed upon finding out he would not be there. George Hamilton didn't have this concern because he's a legend, but I didn't have that luxury." Todd's self-awareness, humility, and keen understanding of entertainment took over. "Something I haven't revealed to too many people is, I took a bit of a grassroots approach to my auditions. The majority, if not all of the audience had arrived at the studio that morning planning on seeing Bob. With this is mind, I arrived at the studio a couple of hours before my call time, parked my car, and walked the line. I started at the front and introduced myself to as many people in line as I could." Todd continued, "I told them who I was and what I was there for. I also told them that they were there on one of the biggest days of my professional life and if they could give me some excitement and energy when I got out on stage I would give them everything I had in return." How did this tactic go over with the crowd? "It worked. When I got out on stage, I now saw familiar faces looking back at me. It put me at ease and created the connection with each contestant that was called up. We all had a blast."

Ultimately, while Todd's two shows went extremely well and the audience loved him, he did not get the job. Neither did the great George Hamilton. As it happened, the actor was not right for the game show atmosphere. While he is a charming and enigmatic actor capable of enchanting a crowd socially, he wasn't a good fit for the game show format and interaction with the contestants. Discussion began to turn toward someone younger and a bit less traditional.

In August of 2007, CBS began airing a new prime time game show called *Power of Ten*, hosted by Drew Carey. At the time, prime time game shows with huge cash prizes were becoming very popular and *Power of Ten* was the latest to shoot for ratings. Carey was very well known as a result of his long-running *The Drew Carey Show*, which finished its run in 2004, and his role as the host of *Whose Line is it Anyway?*, the improvisational comedy show — "The game where everything is made up and the points don't matter." It is widely believed CBS took the opportunity to try and bookend viewership through familiarity. They already had people watching Carey in the evenings, so perhaps those viewers would love to watch him in the mornings as well. The daytime show could fuel the viewership for the prime time show, and vice versa. Soon after the taping of the pilot episode of *Power of Ten*, Drew was approached by CBS to host *Price*. The rest is game show history.

While certainly a little disappointed, Todd was not terribly affected by the decision. "Being one of a handful of hosts to walk through those legendary doors and do what I love to do is something that no one can ever take away from me." Todd continued, as he always has, to be the journeyman entertainer and the go-to guy when a high-quality professional host is in order. The popularity of the live show continued, and Todd hosted the show in between his many television and corporate gigs.

As a host and live entertainer, Todd is absolutely fantastic. He has great timing, both for the games and as a comedic performer. He has a commanding presence on stage that exudes confidence, and he is quite good at using all of these attributes to get the absolute best out of even the most nervous or quiet contestant. You can see how widely affected he is by people like Johnny Carson. His knowledge of the business and of entertainment personalities is extensive. His interviews can be quite brief or in depth depending on what he can draw from the person he is talking to.

I have seen him command the attention of audiences from 500 to 5000. He is a fearless performer, even though he admits to traditional show business nerves. "I get butterflies before every show I do. Thankfully they are the 'I can't wait to get out there and do this' kind as opposed to the 'What did I just get myself into' kind." Todd has full confidence in every movement he makes and every word he utters. He has no problem going out into a crowd of several thousand to bring even more energy to a show. He has been carried, trampled, thrown, manhandled, belched on, and kissed by untold thousands of people, and I think he has had his ass grabbed by contestants at least 1,000 times since I started working with him, which seems to make audiences roar louder.

Todd is a practical joker. He will call crew members and producers on stage, and tell the crowd it's their birthday when it isn't. He has introduced models as being from a town close to where we're playing a show to pander to the crowd, and watch the ladies squirm at the meet-and-greet when people ask which high school they attended. He has smacked me in the crotch while I'm trying to make announcements from backstage, and has introduced me as having a resume any entertainer would love to have. For the record, I have not appeared on *Game of Thrones*, *Better Call Saul*, *Californication*, or *Sons of Anarchy*, nor have I had recurring roles on *Breaking Bad* or *Orange is the New Black*. However, if I ever need a publicist, I believe I will hire Todd, because *everyone believes him.*

Of course, occasionally, his jokes backfire on him He pranked our tour manager one too many times, even after her repeated pleas for him to stop — she is *not* a fan of the limelight. One night, when he was fast asleep in his bunk on the tour bus, she took several rolls of gaffer's tape and completely sealed Todd in his bunk. Hours later, when Todd woke up to go to the bathroom he couldn't get out of his bunk. From the inside, it must have looked perfectly fine as there was the sliding curtain keeping him from the outside world. It just wouldn't *move*. My bunk was across from his, and I got to see look of astonished hysterics when he finally broke through and realized what had happened.

He runs the games masterfully, and there's never been a time when we need more than a tech rehearsal with him. Even though he's fine sharing the stage with me, and welcomes my input and humor, he is the only host I have worked with that makes me completely unnecessary. He has seen every game, heard the copy for every prize, and watched every giveaway there will ever be. His radio background, long career with game shows, and longer career hosting in general have me convinced if I were to actually die on stage, he'd be able to make a great joke out of it and recite prize copy from memory. He's that good.

If there was any doubt as to just how good he is, during a Canadian run in Nova Scotia we had what could only be described as a Hell night regarding the technical aspects of the show. The local sound and lighting crew didn't have the equipment ready or the staff to run the show. The start of the show was delayed by nearly forty-five minutes. Tension in the theatre was evident. Todd grabbed a microphone, and went out on stage to work the crowd and give them an explanation for what was wrong. He went into the crowd and schmoozed his Emmy-winning butt off, doing an incredible twenty-five minutes of off-the-cuff comedy, photo opportunities, crowd-kisses, and reputation-saving.

We hadn't worked together long, when at a fairgrounds show in West Melbourne, Florida, a contestant came to the stage who had been married an astounding 53 years. Todd looked at me and said, "I don't think if you added up all of mine and Andy's marriages combined we'd get close to 53 years!" To which I responded, "Todd, we wouldn't get that close if we cubed them." My quick response gained a laugh from the crowd, and a surprised smile from Todd. I worried I shouldn't have bothered with the line, but it set the tone for our future stage interactions.

Today, I consider Todd to be a very good friend. He's seen me at my best and has been responsible for some of my worst. Like the time he was buying shots, and it turned out that his were water while mine were vodka (I *will* get him for that one!). When I was raising funds for my first book, Todd was one of the first to donate and provide me with an excellent quote for the back cover. He has featured me on his popular podcast, and has always been there to offer professional advice, friendship, and encouragement. In fact, during the writing of this book, he has provided rare photographs, opened a few doors that landed some great interviews, and offered some stories he rarely shares.

While writing this book, I was the first person to hear he had just been nominated again for a Daytime Emmy Award for outstanding game show host. He truly deserves every accolade he receives.

He loves being on the road and on the tour bus with us. "Our live show was once described in a newspaper review as 'part game show, part rock 'n roll concert, and part old time church revival.' I think that's a brilliant way to label what we do."

When asked how he tackles the job of hosting live versions of America's favorite game shows, he offers a perspective that only a journeyman entertainer could have, "Our first priority, obviously, is giving the audience what they want. They want the authentic sets, the music, etc., and we give it to them. But we're also a night out at the theater. Our audience has taken time out of their busy lives, hired babysitters, purchased tickets with hard earned money to come see us and we owe it to them to deliver. The main difference between live shows and television shows is simply the word 'live.' TV shows are limited to just over forty minutes and to the confines of broadcast television. Live shows have ninety minutes to two hours to go out there and have a big game show party. We want people to be talking about the shows long after the last prize has been delivered, and because no two audiences are the same, no two shows will ever be the same. I've often said that everyone who works on live game shows are game show fans first and employees second. That really comes out in the final product."

When asked almost daily why he isn't the host of *Price* on CBS, he replies, "I've hosted Plinko at CBS Television City. And I got to do it not once, but twice! Here we are over ten years later, and thankfully, [*TPIRL*] is bigger and better than I think anyone could have hoped for at the outset. In addition, it's given me the great gift of being able to literally shake hands with tens of thousands of fellow game show fans that, otherwise, I may never have had the opportunity of meeting or working in front of. I'm living the dream!"

....

Todd Newton on:

- **Being a Great Host**

I think a good host is like a good bowl of chili in that it doesn't seem all that complicated, but there are a few "special ingredients" needed to make it really stand out.

First of all, a host must love what he does and who he is doing it for. If you don't love what you're doing you won't have that sparkle in your eye when you're in the middle of it. When I was a host on a major shopping channel, for instance, there were many times I would go back and watch videos of my performance, and cringe. The reason was not that I was bad necessarily, but rather, that I felt no fire about the item I was selling. There was no passion and it showed. True interest cannot be faked.

Another trait a host must possess is the ability to slow down time and really maximize the moment. If a host is rushing or not being truly observant, he or she might miss something crucial. That might be something your guest or contestant says or perhaps it's just a look or a lip quivering. Being fully engaged is crucial to the authenticity of the moment.

Finally, a host needs to be adaptable. You must be able and willing to bend. Bob Eubanks of *The Newlywed Game* once told me, "Remember, you might be the icing but the host is never the whole cake." Truth!

- **Strengths and Weaknesses**

I bring a respect and a passion that is unparalleled. On top of that, I always keep a photo of my kids on me while I'm working. I often look at it moments before walking on stage or on set, and, it just reinforces why I do what I do. I'm a lucky man and I plan to host until I can't host anymore.

- **The Contestants**

I absolutely believe the contestant is the star of the show. That was one of the most valuable pieces of advice Bob Barker ever gave me. He would often remind me that each contestant has a story, a life that they have temporarily put on hold to come play this game. The audience watching, whether it be live or on TV, is watching because they want to root for this person. They want to feel as if they have something invested. Learning the contestants' story is a great way to establish that. Would you rather watch "this woman from Oklahoma" play for a refrigerator or "Nancy from Tulsa who has seven grandchildren under the age of six and has been a walking postal carrier for thirty six years" play for a refrigerator? The difference lies only in the questions the host asks and I am not afraid to ask as many of them as it takes.

In game shows, as in life, the only stupid question is the one that is never asked. I live and work by those words. Every show, every project is an opportunity to enhance lives through maximizing moments of entertainment, information, or inspiration. There is nothing better and it never, ever gets old for me.

- **The Nervous Contestants**

I love 'em up a little bit. I smile, shake their hand and give them a little hug.

- **The Drunk Contestants**

Like Patrick Swayze says in *Roadhouse*, "You may have to ask them to leave. But you will be nice."

- **Not Being Bob Barker or Drew Carey**

Interesting twist to a question I'm still often asked. Peter Tomarken was a great man and a great host. We first met when we both were auditioning for *Whammy!* and he was a complete gentleman.

[*Todd ended up replacing Peter Tomarken*]

If people are initially disappointed by the fact that they aren't seeing Bob or Drew at the live show, all I can do is hope they walk away smiling having had a good time. To be honest, I never really cared all that much. I have incredible respect for Bob but never set out to do an impression of him.

- **Favorite Moments**

I don't single out specific moments, but I do believe in game show magic. We have a lot of opportunity for game show magic [*onstage*].

- **Idols and Influences**

I believe very, very strongly in mentors and coaches. I think if someone is passionate about something, they owe it to themselves and to their craft to seek counsel from as high up the mountain as possible. Legendary game show producer, Sande Stewart is who I credit with igniting my love for the genre when he tapped me to host *Hollywood Showdown* in 1999. I'd never felt so at home in any television setting as I did when I walked onto that stage and experienced the studio audience, the interview of the contestants and the authentic drama of the game play. I just knew it was for me. Sande Stewart continues to serve as my lead counsel as he is my source to game show days gone by — the classic era.

Without question Johnny Carson was my original show business idol. He was the first person I noticed who was on television and entertaining the country by just being himself — albeit a slightly exaggerated version. I then began to take notice of Dick Clark, Richard Dawson, Bob [*Barker*] and many others. But more than anything I watched the master [*Barker*] himself. I watched what he did when the camera wasn't on him and what measures he took to establish that rapport with the contestant that is so vital. Soon I mustered up the courage to ask to meet with him after a taping and he graciously obliged. We had an instant connection through both our love and respect of game shows and for the great city of St. Louis [*Todd's home town*]. I'm grateful for our friendship and for the many days I had the opportunity to sit in his famed WGMC [*World's Greatest Master of Ceremonies*] director's chair and learn from him.

I'm a big fan of the P.T. Barnum style of self-promotion and hustle. No one will be a bigger cheerleader for you than you will be for yourself, so in that regard, I have great respect for people like Paul Stanley and Gene Simmons of KISS.

Personally, my work ethic stems from watching my father. He was, and is, a true workhorse who believes in earning every dollar and never taking any opportunity for granted. He is also a risk taker and I've certainly inherited some of that.

....

Todd Newton is the Emmy Award-winning host of Family Game Night which appears on The Hub, the co-host of Monopoly Millionaire's Club alongside comedian, Billy Gardell, and he owns his own successful realty company in Arizona.

SEVEN

....

JERRY SPRINGER

"We are intrigued by how human beings behave. There is nothing that has ever been on any of our [*television*] shows that isn't already in the Bible, that isn't already in Shakespeare, that isn't already in Milton, and in all the great works."

- Jerry Springer

....

In show business, name recognition is everything. Few entertainers have managed to be immediately recognizable to the general public by the utterance of a single name. Madonna, Cher, and Prince have achieved this by being incredible performers and clever marketing. Others are instantly identifiable by last name such as Carson, Sullivan, or Letterman.

I dare say there are two entertainers equally identified by first, last, or full name: Bette Midler and Jerry Springer. When you hear "Springer or "Jer-ry, Jer-ry, Jer-ry" chanted anywhere, there is no doubt that Jerry Springer is in the house. Much the same way Jerry can reference the Bible, Shakespeare, or Milton, the world can reference Springer and with almost universal recognition. Love him or hate him, Jerry Springer is an institution.

In November of 2011, it was announced Jerry Springer would be coming to Vegas. Being originally from the Chicago area, I was very familiar with Springer. I remember watching him in the very early days, when The *Jerry Springer Show* aspired to be like *Donahue*. Back then, my parents were excited to see Springer coming to Chicago. They both went to college in Oxford, Ohio, near Cincinnati and were very curious to see what the former Cincy mayor had to offer the airwaves.

Interestingly, I was supposed to meet and work with Springer long before I ever became associated with the world's most famous game show. Soon after I moved to Las Vegas in 2007, I received a phone call from *The Jerry Springer Show* wanting me to be a regular performer. At that time, they were using circus acts as a backdrop for some of the more outrageous guest stories. Whenever the tales sounded like they were part of the circus, jugglers, acrobats, and clowns would stroll behind as the crowd chanted Jerry's name. They wanted me to spin plates and juggle along with the other performers. I would have *loved* for that to happen. Of course, until I knew for sure that

this was a real job offer, I confess I was worried that someone from my past wanted to confront me on national television. I've received a lot of phone calls as an entertainer
in 30 years, but when you get a call from *The Jerry Springer
Show*, you do tend to do a little homework before signing
on the dotted line. As it happened, they had been under
the impression that I was still living in Chicago at the
time, and didn't want to fly me out from Vegas every time
they needed a plate-spinner. I referred them to a friend
who spun plates for many of their shows.

If I remember correctly, it was either Bob Goen or Joey
Fatone who was hosting when I first officially met Jerry.
He was brought to Vegas to get a general idea of how the
show flowed on stage. I was backstage waiting to go on
when our executive producer tapped my shoulder and introduced me to Jerry.

Jerry is a relatively soft-spoken, friendly, and charming
man. He is also polite, extremely intelligent, and he rarely
greets people without a smile or a joke. If I could choose
one word to describe Jerry Springer as a person, I would
choose *avuncular,* because he truly is like America's uncle.
He is approachable, affable, and kind, which made the
thought of him hosting a game show completely logical.
If nothing else, it sounded like an idea worth trying out if
a little outrageous. I asked him what his first reaction was
when he was asked to host a family game show. Mimicking a phone call, he replied, "Who is this anyway? What's

the punch line?" With a laugh, he said, "It wasn't that surprising to do this show. It all was a consequence of what I had done before. I was on *Dancing with the Stars. That* was a shocker. The reaction to me being on that show turned out to be good. Because of that appearance and the public response, NBC offered me the job of hosting *America's Got Talent.* They [*NBC*] said, 'Oh, he really can appeal to Middle America and not just the crazy people. He can work the mainstream.' After I couldn't do the '09 season [*due to a run on Broadway*] they asked if I would do the live tour of *America's Got Talent,* which is produced by the same people who produce popular live game shows, so I got this job because they were happy with what I was doing on *America's Got Talent.* It wasn't *way* out of the blue to go from my show to game shows."

I was eager to start working with Jerry. If for no other reason than to have a photo with him for my Facebook page.

Once again, my moment to work with Jerry Springer was delayed when I was told that I wouldn't be announcing for the Springer dates in Las Vegas. This was to be Jerry's first time hosting the show. Since he was arguably the biggest star to host the program, they wanted one of their more experienced announcers to helm the microphone. I was also told that Jerry likes to be a lot more aloof when hosting a program. Whether it is his own show, his current game show, *Baggage,* or any other loosely-scripted program, he keeps something of a professional distance from the show. In a game show setting, it would be the job of the announcer to help keep him on track and make sure the game flowed properly. Daniel Rosen was brought in for the inaugural Jerry Springer dates. I understood the decision, but that didn't mean I wasn't disappointed I didn't want or need the four weeks off, and I had the awful feeling that I never *really* had the job. That's show biz

The schedule worked out so that I had two weeks off, Thanksgiving week back on with Bob Goen hosting, and then another two weeks off so Jerry could finish his run. The upside was spending Thanksgiving on stage and serving "a sumptuous repast" to Bob. The downside was being out a month's worth of pay and wondering if I'd be asked back. These were trial dates for Springer, and nobody knew if Jerry was going to host any more.

The initial Springer dates came and went, to the delight of the producers and audience members, and things got back to the regular rotation of hosts. By 2012, there were more Springer dates announced, and this time I was considered seasoned enough to be his announcer.

When Jerry was brought backstage, and I went to re-introduce myself to him. After shaking his hand, before I could get a word out, Jerry said, "I remember you. We've met once before. Your name is Andy, right?" Now, I realize the producers certainly could have told him the names of who he would be working with, but I saw him do the exact same thing with other people on the crew, people he'd met only once. Jerry Springer is the type of man who makes a point to remember people. I think that says a lot about a man who deals with thousands of people every year. Perhaps it's the politician in him, but it's an amazing quality.

My boss pulled me aside prior to the show. "You can't go on auto-pilot for a moment, Andy. I have never seen you do that, of course, but please remain in the moment, every moment, of the shows. Jerry is not like our other hosts."

Our executive producer was there to ensure everything went smoothly. Of course, in this instance, he was also concerned whether things would go well with me. "Andy, how well do you *know* the games?" he asked. I told him I knew them by heart. "Would you please go over the game rules for me?" Without hesitation, I went through the rules with ease and nailed them all. I asked why there was so much concern about the rules, and he told me that I would now become the Keeper of the Rules whenever Jerry hosted because of his aloof style of hosting a show.

One of the reasons Jerry is beloved by American audiences is how he hosts his program. With all of the craziness and outrageous behavior exhibited on his show, he is never viewed as the one deserving of blame or scrutiny, he is merely the Ringmaster. He achieves this by being a genuinely friendly man who is truly interested in people; he disassociates himself from the show he is hosting. "It's all in the cards," he said.

Jerry purposefully knows *nothing* about the guests appearing on his show. He may know the subject of that day's program, but he doesn't want to know anything about the secrets that will be revealed. His ever present blue cards contain little more than names and a statement or two for him to read. "Sitting here now is Elsie from Georgia. Elsie has come here to tell us something very interesting about her family." That is pretty much *all* Jerry knows about his guests. Jerry is able to take those names and notes, and with charm and an innate ability to get people talking, draws compelling entertainment out of anyone. That is how he hosts every show he works on. He likes the spontaneous nature of interacting with the people and he doesn't want to lose any of that excitement. So, when he began hosting game shows, he wanted general knowledge of the games written down on cards for him. The cards are almost a trademark for him, and he relies on them to guide him from start to finish. Which is why I needed to know the games well. So that I could keep Jerry in the moment, and keep our games, brand, and reputation intact.

The first few shows we worked together, I did my old job as announcer and my new job as Keeper of the Rules well. There were times I felt he was lost or confused by what was going on around him. Now that I have worked with him often, and spoken with him about this, I realize he was utilizing another shrewd bit of business that only he could get away with.

Much like on his own show, he lets the moment drive his reactions. He refers to those cards for guidance, and when the crazy comes out to play, he takes time to let his natural sense of humor diffuse the awkward moments. He *loves* giving the audience a reason to think he's lost on the show. He once told me that by giving the appearance of being as surprised as the audience, it endears him more to the viewers and brings out the best in the guests. He is also keen to point out that the contestants and the audience know the show so well, they won't let him stray far from the path. For him, it's about the people more than the games. "It's almost like the rules are secondary to the entertainment factor. That's just the backdrop," Springer explains. "It's really just an excuse to get regular people on stage and see how they interact. It's not like we really care what the price of the cereal bowl is. It's that we love to see the person grapple with it, with success and failure, and 'Oh, I'm nervous'. That's the entertainment in the show."

I have worked with him many times now. He is certainly more familiar with the games than when he started, and he's quite clear on the rules. He uses his Jerry-centric traits to keep the audience engaged, create moments of levity other hosts may not get to enjoy, and when it is all over, people walk away still feeling they got a proper game show experience. A somewhat altered one, but the show and its long traditions remain safe and sound, held within the hearts and minds of our viewers.

Jerry doesn't view a presentation as game show tradition, but rather as a modern-day form of Vaudeville. "These tours of the iconic shows, where you work with a live audience, where there's obviously no script, and you're picking people at random to be contestants creates an inter-audience/entertainer interaction that you just don't have in any other form of show business. Every show gets to be unique. Comedy presents itself with every new guest, every new circumstance or question. It's fun! I love doing it." There are many unusual moments when the show is hosted by Jerry. Whenever a trip to Las Vegas comes up as a prize, he breaks into an Elvis song. Yes, Jerry Springer sings! He is probably the only host who will actively make fun of the grocery items, the prizes, and some of the most iconic games. He has even gone into his own pocket a few times when a guest has lost a game entirely. I can recall several occasions when someone was unlucky enough to get a big ole zero with every effort to win, and Jerry opened his wallet and gave the contestant a hundred bucks. "I never want any of these people to feel bad for losing." Unfortunately, the rules don't allow for things like that, so he doesn't do that anymore.

People tell Jerry things they would *never* tell anyone else, let alone on a microphone in a room with 2,500 people in it. We once had a contestant from Virginia get on stage who was very excited to be on the show and particularly excited to meet Jerry. Jerry asked the lady what brought her to Vegas.

She could have said she was on vacation.

She could have said she was in town for business.

She could have said she was visiting family.

She very loudly proclaimed, "My husband and I want to have sex in all fifty states!" As you can imagine, this brought about a most stunned, and loud, response from the crowd. The woman covered her face as she realized what she had just said. Jerry, took a moment to allow her to compose herself, then asked, "Well, how long have you been married?" She said they'd been together 20 years. Jerry said, "I *have* to ask . . . what's the total up to now?" She loudly replied, "*Two!*" The theater erupted with laughter.

After locating the husband in the audience, Jerry shrugged his shoulders and said, "Listen, sir, you really need to step up your game. I'd have been a hero in the Colonies!" Without a doubt, the crowd response was among the loudest spontaneous roars of applause and laughter I have ever heard. This is what makes him an unorthodox, but excellent host. You will not get the show you may have been expecting, but you will be thoroughly entertained.

....

Jerry Springer on:

- **Being a Great Host**

I think the key is to stay out of the way of the natural personality of the person you are talking with. Whether it's on my show or on *America's Got Talent*, whatever shows we do, as long as I can stay out of the way of who is on stage, then we have a chance of having an entertaining show.

- **Strengths and Weaknesses**

Entertainment has never been my passion.

- **The Contestants**

Nobody is coming to the show to see me. Regardless of the notoriety of the name, the fact is, what ultimately is entertaining is seeing these contestants up here. I love the idea of live entertainment working with regular people. People who aren't famous and who aren't trying to sell a book or a movie. It's just human beings interacting. That is the most exciting part of show business that I can find.

- ## The Nervous Contestants

There's some element of it [*when we watch the contestants*], even though we say, "that's not me," when, in fact, if we were up there, it would be us. We kind of know we would get nervous. From the moment I look in the mirror, before going out there, I realize [*laughing*] I am never any better than the people I'm in front of. So, I am always talking with equals.

- ## Not Being Bob Barker or Drew Carey

The only way it works . . . it would not work if I would try to be like Bob Barker. Everyone would say, "What's Jerry trying to be like Bob Barker for? He doesn't talk like that." So, the only way anything ever works, is if you're authentic.

I never feel any pressure to do it like someone else does it, because, that's not going to work. I just do it as I would do a show, which is joking around. I've found with any job I've had, as long as I behave as I normally behave, and don't try to fake it, people just smile and say, "Ahhh, that's just Jerry!" I probably get away with a lot of jokes that someone else who is more proper or a traditional game show host would not. You could get another host who could say some of the things I say, and the people would ask "What's he doing?" With me, they say, "Ohhh, that's Jerry!" So, don't try to pretend to be someone you're not. You can't fake it for an hour and a half. At some point, they're going to see the cracks.

- **Favorite Moments**

On every show, there's at least one contestant that is just a great personality. Funny for all kinds of reasons. Sometimes it is pure comedy and other times it is rather poignant. Like yesterday, when a contestant who had some challenges, and the way everyone just warmed up to him and rooted for him. That's a wonderful moment. How many times in his life will he have the opportunity for people to cheer for him? When you realize you are a part of that, how cool is that?

- **Idols and Influences**

I was born in England and I came to America when I was five. I started the first grade in a New York school. Because of my accent, because of the way my mother dressed me as a little British boy in a blue suit, shorts, the jacket, bow tie, a beret, and knee socks . . . the kids beat the crap out of me. You build up a defense mechanism and I realized if I could have kids laughing, they would like me. It's harder to swing at someone if you're laughing.

....

Jerry Springer is the host of the wildly popular The Jerry Springer Show as well as the host of Baggage on the Game Show Network.

EIGHT

....

JD ROBERTO

"The truth is, we're not curing cancer, here. We're not feeding the homeless or building homes in the third world. As professions go, game show host ranks pretty high on the fluff meter. So it becomes that much more important to be a generous, decent, kind person on stage, on-air, and, most importantly, in your day-to-day life."

- JD Roberto

....

Coincidentally, the two hosts I knew the least about prior to working with them have hosted the same television show. JD Roberto has enjoyed a busy career in entertainment as a host, announcer, stunt man, actor, and writer. Game show fans will know him as the announcer for Game Show Network's *The Pyramid*, the host of Animal Planet's *You Lie Like a Dog* and Food Network's *Food Fight*. Most prominently, he was host of the very popular *Shop 'til You Drop*, a show originally hosted by Pat Finn. For a brief time, he was the announcer for

The Price is Right on CBS during its 39th season. Quite a resume indeed.

Roberto is also something of a big branch in the game show family tree. "I started working on *TPIRL* in Atlantic City. The original producer, Andy Felsher and I had worked together many years ago on the same job where Andy met Jeff Palmer, who would eventually replace Felsher," according to JD.

As an announcer, I enjoyed his work. He has a clear and striking baritone voice, and a considerably different approach to the audience warm up from other announcers. JD told me, "As a live show announcer, you warm up the audience and really set the tone for the evening. You've really got to have a sense of your crowd. That's both the thrill and challenge of a live show."

I have only worked with JD for a week's worth of shows, but I felt as though I knew him long before he'd arrived for duty Everybody backstage was happy to see JD; he is a well-liked guy. Seeing how he was being received by the crew made me all the more eager to get on stage and see how he hosts the show.

As an announcer, you need to watch the host and wait to see where you may fit in the dynamic. Before rehearsal, JD pulled me aside to let me know that if I had any good jokes and recognized an appropriate moment to chime in with said joke or comment, I was more than welcome to do so. He also wanted to warn me that if I had any really good lines, they would likely live on in other shows he did. "Steal, steal, steal. Hear a great one liner? Steal it. See a great moment? Steal it. Of course, I mean that in the best possible way. In the end you try to put on the best show you can for the audience. If some other host has a great way to raise the bar, you owe it to the audience to deliver it."

He likes the back-and-forth interaction between the host and the announcer. "The announcer on a live show has vastly more freedom to chat and banter than on a TV show," JD said. "That's really the nature of a live show in general."

As a host, JD manages to run the show at a brisk pace without losing any of the magic that can happen on stage. He is wonderful with the contestants and does a superb job of bringing the absolute best out of everyone. His on-stage energy is excellent, and he almost dares the crowd *not* to have fun. While I know every live performer has had tough crowds, I can't imagine any crowd being too tough for JD. "You tailor your material and your energy to the room. A Tuesday 2 PM show in Branson isn't going to be the same group of people as an 8 PM Saturday night show in Las Vegas."

I appreciated his need to get the crowd to recognize me. Even though we hadn't worked together previously, he directed the crowd the give a round of applause for "the best announcer in the business, Andy Martello." I know it was a show business thing to say but I told him after the show I was going to steal that line and put it on my press kit.

Show biz niceties aside, after he got some applause for the announcer, he started into a classic "How are you? How have you been?" kind of dialogue with me. None of the other hosts had ever done this with me before, and I enjoyed that little moment in the show. It set a great tone for the crowd. It implied we were long-time friends, and gave the impression our stage show was more than a job. It told the crowd that we were a family.

That family feeling allowed for memorable moments between the two of us without stopping the flow or pace of the show. "Not every announcer is able to banter in a way that makes the show fun and interesting, I don't do it with everyone," JD said. "Having been an announcer myself, I know how to get the most out of the guy behind the podium when I am hosting. Honestly, it takes some of the pressure off when you've got a great announcer, and when both the host and the announcer are in sync, the show is that much better."

I value my time onstage with JD. He has never hesitated to answer an e-mail or return a phone call, and he is another perfect example of a rare, true gentleman in entertainment.

....

JD Roberto On:

- **Being a Great Host**

Hosting is a real art form all its own. That might sound very flowery and self-important, but just remember all the times some celeb or comedian was tapped to host a show and how many times it went horribly wrong, and you'll get a sense of what I mean. Some people can do it. Wayne Brady and Richard Dawson come to mind as comedians and actors who moved seamlessly into hosting. Like most things, it's not nearly as simple as it looks.

In game shows there's a really fun, challenging balance of being completely in the moment with the contestant, really watching and listening and making sure you're getting their very best, while at the same time playing traffic cop. You've got to get the rules out there without sounding boring and dry, you've got to build the drama but know when to move along. You've got to manage the show's running time (a commercial break is always right around the corner), but still know when the slow things down and have a great moment with a player. You're part producer, part actor, part best friend all at the same time.

- **Strengths and Weaknesses**

Okay, false modesty aside here goes: I'm good on the fly. That's probably my biggest strength in a live show, whatever you throw at me I'm going to be able to handle and find a way to have fun with it. Honestly, I prefer working live for exactly that reason. There are guys who are slicker and smoother than I will ever be, and there are guys that are more handsome and more stylish. I'm quick-witted, and I love people and that serves me well in what I do on TV, but it especially lets me shine in a live show environment.

- **The Contestants**

Mostly, it boils down to being able to make the person standing next to you the star of the show. Maybe that means asking great, interesting questions to a celebrity guest on a talk show, maybe it means helping Mabel from Des Moines come out of her shell on the big stage in Las Vegas. The more you give away the spotlight to your guest or your constant, the more you both shine.

- **The Nervous Contestants**

A nervous contestant is a lot of fun, actually. You have them do some deep breathing, get the audience to chant their name, make them dance a little bit — anything to break the tension and help them settle into the experience. From their point of view, it's all happening so fast, it's hard to really be in the moment.

- **The Drunk Contestants**

Get them on and off as quick as you can [*smiles*].

- **Not Being Bob Barker or Drew Carey**

Hosting is all about remembering that the star of the show is the game itself. Make the show shine and you'll shine. That's always been my approach and it works every time.

I've never experienced an audience that was expecting Bob or Drew. But, I've been flown in a couple of times to replace or fill in for bigger names. Joey Fatone and Jerry Springer come to mind. You get a little nervous going out there knowing that some die-hard Springer fans paid to see Jerry, and now you're going to have to win them over. But that's what you do. You go out and do a great show. Make them laugh, keep it moving, you do a great show and entertain the hell out of them. I've had a couple of people whine and moan before the show that I wasn't the guy they were expecting, but I've had thousands of people come up to me afterward and tell me how much fun they had at the show. That's what matters.

[*When asked to compare this experience to his experience taking over for Pat Finn*]

Interesting question. *Shop 'til You Drop* is an interesting story. Pat Finn gave me one of my first on-camera jobs in Los Angeles. He's a talented, sweet man who, in addition to a successful career on camera and stage, has run a production company for decades. I did work as a producer and host for everything from infomercials to MTV reality shows for his company. Years after I first met and worked for Pat, I got a call asking if I'd be interested in hosting the all new *Shop 'til You Drop*. I immediately called him and said "Pat, someone just called and offered me your job," and he laughed and said "Yeah, I knew they were out looking for someone new. I'm glad it's you, at least the money is going to someone I like." That's the kind of guy Pat is; not just a great talent, but a great person. In the end we did something like 200 episodes of the all new *Shop 'til You Drop*. But I still love Pat's version of the show.

- **Favorite Moments**

I've had so many incredible moments it's hard to pick just one. Bachelor parties, big wins, lifelong fans getting on stage and nearly fainting. It doesn't happen with every contestant every day but it's hard to get through a show without at least one really special person or experience.

- **Idols and Influences**

Probably a lot of people the average person has never heard of. I'm a fan of Mike Richards who runs *TPIR*. He's an example of a guy with vision and an incredible work ethic. Pat Finn, who gave me my first job in Los Angeles when I moved there many years ago. Steve Grant, and Bob Loudin, game show directors who taught me the business of game show and, more importantly, taught me patience and perspective on a set. Anyone who has shown simple humility, kindness and had a sense of humor about themselves.

Jobs come and go, shows burst onto the scene and then tank. That's our very fickle business. My influences are all great people first and great professionals second. I don't always succeed at either but, in the end, that's what I aspire to be.

....

JD Roberto was most recently the co-host of the nationally syndicated morning talk show, The Better Show and the host of DailyBurn.com's Your Daily Burn 365.

NINE

DAVID RUPRECHT

"Next time you're at the checkout and you hear the beep, think of the fun you could be having on Supermarket Sweep!"

....

For thirteen years, television audiences around the country heard David Ruprecht say that familiar phrase.

Supermarket Sweep was never one of my favorite shows. When I learned I would be working with David in Branson, Missouri, many of my friends called and e-mailed me freaking out with excitement, and I realized that I had somehow missed an all-time classic. It seemed I was not the only Andy who was not a huge fan of the show. Ruprecht's agent contacted Andy Felsher about the possibility of Dave landing a host and announcer job for one of Fremantle's live shows. "It was, apparently, a bit of a tough sale because Felsher was never a fan of *Supermarket Sweep*. He didn't like the fact that the bonus round (The Sweep) could not be 'played' by the home audience. Luckily, Andy tried me once in Atlantic City and the audiences turned out to be *much* bigger fans of *Sweep* than Andy.

I was very nervous to meet and work with Dave. I'd only heard great things about the guy, but I was worried there might be some sort of animosity or confrontation when we met since I had essentially replaced Ruprecht on a show he had worked for many years. There were a few folks considered to be regular announcers, but to the best of my knowledge, Dave was the only one who had bought property in Vegas because of the job. Every week for nearly five years, he announced the show four days a week, usually with Todd Newton hosting. On the fifth day, he would host while Todd worked his speaking and corporate engagements. The crowds got a full helping of game show history with Newton and Ruprecht onstage, and the show was a success. Rather suddenly, and soon after he had purchased a home, he was informed that the show was making a few changes, the announcer being one of them. A few auditions later, a new guy — some unknown kid with no game show or warm up experience — ended up taking his place.

Nobody likes to lose a job, particularly in the entertainment business. I was very concerned there would be a little resentment between us. It's not like I stole the gig from him. It was a classic "that's show biz" moment which serves as a reminder to everyone how fickle and brutal this business can be. I tend to overthink these things, but since he was getting paid way more than I was for this weekend maybe that would smooth things over. The weekend turned out to be a bit sudden, and certainly awkward, but more than amicable.

Before being scheduled for Branson, I had been booked to perform several shows in Canada. I started that tour intending to be on the road for nine weeks, and I was enjoying being back on the road. The energy and excitement was so much different and more frenzied than residency shows. A few days into the tour, I was told there was a chance they would be using a different announcer for the Canadian dates. About two weeks later, it was confirmed. This was a bit heartbreaking, but that's show biz. As a consolation prize, they offered me the show dates in Branson. Not only would I be able to recoup some of the money I would be losing, but I could see some beautiful country, perform the show I loved, and work with another new host . . . provided Dave didn't stab me in the eye or something.

As it happened, I was worried for nothing. He was every bit as friendly and outgoing as Todd had described. Our humor and demeanor were an excellent fit, and it wasn't long before we were exchanging jokes and talking like old war buddies. Plus, Dave is a cigar smoker, so we had that in common. We also have many mutual friends, so our conversations came fast and without any awkwardness.

Bob Goen always had the best opening line whenever he would host shows in Branson. "We're the only show in Branson without the word 'jamboree' in the title." The Lawrence Welk Theater is a beautiful showroom, with state-of-the art equipment and an excellent team of people making the show look great. The crowds, however, were not the excitable, screaming fans running rampant with crazed enthusiasm. It was a much older demographic, and the showroom was far too large for the crowds we were drawing, so sometimes it felt as though we were performing in a cave. Of course, a lot of that changed when the familiar theme music would start and the games got underway.

I noticed the calculated way Dave Ruprecht works. Even though he had done game shows for years, he was very meticulous, making notes in his script and practicing his lines well before we started rehearsal. He liked to work out every detail of the show, prop placement, timing, and dialogue and try his best to eliminate any surprises along the way. I have been told he was the same as an announcer, writing notes and symbols down on the script to accent his speech, push certain inflections and cadences, and punch the big prizes.

Dave has a very soothing, down-home voice that fits in well with the Branson atmosphere and age has given him the appearance of a kindly southern gentleman. That also went a long way with the Branson crowds. Even with the older, less game show-centric crowd, the audience connected with Dave quite well and there were many fans of *Supermarket Sweep* at every show.

There wasn't a lot of interaction between us on stage, but the show ran smoothly with a bit of a laid back feeling.

I enjoyed watching the rehearsals as much as the shows, in part because Dave is such a perfectionist. He wants to get every word, every bit of business, and every rule or piece of dialogue out just right. He had not worked some of the games in quite some time, so it was comical to watch him working out the notes and lines in his head. I don't know why he was worried. Being the professional he is, the games went without a hitch every time.

Dave Ruprecht is easily one of the most pleasant people I have had the pleasure to work with. He was kind enough to show me around Branson, and point out a few favorite places to eat and enjoy the scenery. We shared a few drinks and cigars during our weekend, and there was no doubt that smiling face looking back at me belonged to a friend.

....

David Ruprecht On:

- **Being a Great Host**

Google "Todd Newton!" Todd Newton is indisputably the best in the business! I have never seen anyone who could take a "blah" contestant and turn them into solid gold like Todd.

Keeping the show running quickly and smoothly is very important. Most importantly, remember you are *not* the star, the contestants are.

- **Strengths and Weaknesses**

I think one of the nicest compliments I ever got was from Cathy Dawson who said, "You actually *like* the people, and it shows." The ongoing popularity of *Sweep* didn't hurt either.

- **The Contestants**

It's important to never put down the contestants or be negative. Make the contestants the stars.

- **Not Being Bob Barker or Drew Carey**

I never felt any audience disappointment. By the time Randy West or JD or Daniel Rosen had warmed them up and they showed my intro reel, the audience was always

with me 100%. It helped that *Supermarket Sweep* still reso-
nated with so many people.

- **Favorite Moments**

My first stint with Fremantle's live shows was in Atlantic City, and it was a bit nerve-racking at first. Thank
heavens I had great friend John Ricci and soon-to-be great
friend Scott Reside teach me the ropes expertly. So nerve-
racking, my first night I sleep-walked for the first time in
my life and woke up in the hotel hallway. Next night I got
smart and put my room key in the sweats I sleep in. Unfortunately, the next night I sleep-walked and woke up in
the hotel hallway as naked as the day I was born.

- **Idols and Influences**

Obviously I went to school on the Master, Todd Newton. Some Hosts, like Goen, taught me I don't have to
push with the energy etc. Some, I learned what *not* to do.
It was always a pleasure though being Host or Announcer.

....

*David Ruprecht has been seen recently in popular television
programs such as Cold Case, The Bold and the Beautiful, and
True Blood. He also has appeared on the Broadway stage.*

TEN

PAT FINN

"The best hosts on game shows are the ones who are confidently having fun themselves."

- Pat Finn

···

P at is best known as the long-time host of the popular *Shop 'til You Drop*, but game show fans know his national break came in 1990 when he was chosen to host the remake of *The Joker's Wild*, replacing the great Jack Barry. I first worked with Pat Finn in 2013 in Prior Lake, Minnesota, where we were getting ready to embark on another big tour. It was both refreshing, and a little off-putting, to learn a new host was coming on board. Touring is a lot different from residency shows. You need someone who is available for the dates, but who is also ready (and willing) to live on a tour bus. That person had better be easy to get along with as well, or life for everyone on the bus would be very tense. Thankfully, Pat was both available and affable. He also had some history with the world's most famous game show.

"I was being considered as host of the nighttime version of *TPIR* back in the 90's, but Lifetime wouldn't let me do it with my exclusive contract for *Shop 'til You Drop*. So, when I heard of the live show years later, I was immediately interested. At first they had all the good hosts they needed so nothing happened. Then my close friend Mark Walberg, who was one of the hosts on the live tour, couldn't do certain dates because of conflicts with his *Antiques Roadshow* schedule so he suggested me," Pat said. "Mark really went to bat for me because he knew my Mom had just died, and he thought it would be a good distraction. He was right. It was a blast!

I think one of the reasons Pat and I got along was because he went through an eerily similar audition process to land this job. "I played some of the games in a conference room for the powers that be and they liked what I did, so I got booked to go on the tour for a few weeks."

He is a tall, fit man, with a stoic nature. While he certainly enjoys himself and has a good time, he reminds me of John Wayne in *The Quiet Man*. I knew his television credentials, and of his work as a producer and director, but I had no idea how long it had been since he had hosted a show of any kind, much less a live show.

Pat is easily the most soft-spoken of the hosts I've worked with, with the possible exception of Drew Lachey. He has an almost Zen quality to how he carries himself and interacts with others. More often than not, I got the impression that he was perfectly content quietly observing the conversations around him before adding anything to them. *If*, in fact, he chose to add something to the conversation. It's this ability to focus and listen that makes him a good host.

The shows at the Mystic Lake Casino would be his first with the live audience, and everyone but the spectators in the house could tell he was a little nervous. He relied upon me a great deal during those first few shows to keep him on point. I remember him telling me ahead of time that he would likely count on me to make sure he didn't stray from the path. The shows went well, and soon his fears were alleviated. He did what all great hosts do so well, he won over the audience with endearing charm and professionalism.

Pat is generous with his stage time, something I always appreciate. He frequently referred to me for game rules, to ask questions and start conversations for interaction, and checked with me often for reassurance that he was on track. "I think anytime people can see a real human connection between people who genuinely like and respect each other on stage, it feels more interesting. For example, in my opinion, the Jerry Seinfeld and Larry David interaction was one of the best parts of the SNL 40th anniversary special. Besides, you know the show far better than me, so it was great to know you always have my back." The stage is not the only place where Pat Finn is a very giving individual.

Pat was very much a part of the team, and in many ways, he may be the most generous of all the hosts I've worked with. Not generous in the gift-giving or the drink-buying sense, but rather as a person who truly cares about the happiness and success of others.

For several weeks, Pat had made a point to get to know everyone. Not just their names, but their likes and dislikes, the names of family members, and everyone's life goals. He is the kind of man who takes an interest in the people around him. One member of our crew, Kyle Hays, had mentioned to Pat he was an aspiring country singer/songwriter. Kyle is a very talented guy and definitely has an excellent voice. At the time, he did not have a plan to record a demo or take the dream a little farther down the road. He was content singing at his local bar and earning occasional tips from the patrons. Pat took great interest in Kyle's dream, and asked him to play his guitar and sing a song he wrote.

Pat checked the calendar for our next stretch of days off. He mentioned them to Kyle, and encouraged him to get a demo recording done. He even went so far as to offer to reserve some studio space at his own expense for this purpose. After a shocked, "Are you serious?" discussion, Kyle agreed to give it a shot.

We were approaching some dates near Tunica, Mississippi, and had a few days off along the way. Being so close to Memphis, TN, I was rounding up a group to grab a dinner at the Rendezvous for delicious ribs. Pat made arrangements for Kyle to record a demo of one of his songs and have it professionally mixed at a studio in Memphis, and we decided to make it a family outing. We would be in studio with Kyle for his recording session, shoot some video for him in case he wanted to make a basic music video for the song, then head out for a meal. Dinner and a show as it were.

Truthfully, I think we were all interested to see if both Pat and Kyle would actually go through with it. Kyle was still in shock that a relative stranger would take such an interest in him, much less rent studio space on his behalf. We all were. That amazement increased when we realized that Pat hadn't booked some tiny recording studio or called in a favor from a friend with equipment in his garage. No, we found ourselves in the hallowed halls of Ardent Studios in Memphis, where Stevie Ray Vaughn, Robert Cray, ZZ Top, Bob Dylan, Cheap Trick, and countless other legendary acts have recorded million-selling songs since 1967.

Kyle laid down some basic tracks, and then we gathered in a different room to record his music video. I have to say, it was great fun for all of us, especially Kyle.

After the studio time was up, we planned to head to Rendezvous for dinner. Pat, quietly chose to stay behind and finish up some work, but he did it with a big grin on his face. He was happy to help someone he liked take a big step toward realizing a dream. Whether or not Kyle Hays would go on to become a singing sensation, at least he now *knew* a little bit of what it would take to realize that dream. That's the kind of person Pat Finn is. I don't know what became of that demo single, but I do know that of all our hosts, Pat Finn is the one with the biggest heart.

....

Pat Finn on:

- **Being a Great Host**

You need to be fully present, be in control, accountable for everything that happens, which I suppose goes for hosting anything. A live show has more adrenaline because you can't just stop tape and do a take two. There's more energy with a crowd of 2000 people than the 200 at a TV taping, yet less pressure because it's all about having fun!

- ### Strengths and Weaknesses

I think my biggest strength is that I truly get excited for the players and I can talk while my brain is thinking of the next thing to say or do. Looking like what people think of as a game show host image doesn't hurt either. I have learned to use the energy of a live audience more. On TV, mostly it was about connecting with the home viewer. The studio audience was just there for background noise. During a few seasons of *Shop 'til You Drop* we didn't even have a live audience, we just had someone with a keyboard playing different levels of applause and laughter and he would add the sound as we taped live. Now, I can see the live audience being a more important part of the show.

- ### The Contestants

Connect with the players and make them the stars.

- ### The Nervous Contestants

Look them in the eye and talk to them, not talk to the audience about them. Touch their arm or shoulder occasionally. Care.

- ### The Drunk Contestants

I help the audience laugh. Just have fun and make it a wild party where your friend is having too much fun but everyone is enjoying it.

- ### Not Being Bob Barker or Drew Carey

I have always been a fan of Bob Barker so I can hear his voice in my head out there sometimes. I can honestly say that I have never thought about that for *Joker's Wild*, I just do the best job being me and audiences seem to appreciate it. Were there any traditional showbiz nerves at a live show? I was more concerned that I would do as well as the other hosts so they would ask me back, which they have many times. Before my original conference room audition, I was coached by my friend and colleague John Ricci in addition to producing TV game shows for my company and for others, so I got some good tips.

- **Favorite Moments**

There are so many great moments with the shows. Highlights include how the entire crew in Branson, MO would always gather right before I stepped out on stage and would scream, high five, and cheer me on. Also, the connection with the rest of the cast and crew that happens on the road. When you finish a taping in L.A., everyone goes their separate ways, but on the road, we get to hang out and connect as friends.

- **Idols and Influences**

I grew up watching Jack Barry and Bob Barker, so to have had the chance to do their shows has been a really blessing.

....

Here's Your Host!

Pat Finn is a successful business man and owner of Results Pro-
ducers, a television production company.

ELEVEN

....

GEORGE GRAY

"I've never been delusional about my celebrity status. In fact, I think they are scraping the bottom of the barrel by the time they call me for a job. However, the people who come to see a live show are true die-hard fans. They may want to see Drew Carey on stage. Failing that, I, as the ugly, redheaded stepchild make a great second choice. It's a great fit and a total blast!"

- George Gray

....

George Gray is a perfect representation of just about everything and everyone I have described in this book so far, especially the *fun*. In many ways, George has many of the best traits of every host I have worked with, while bringing his own unique style to the mix. I am certain he could provide some tales of debauchery when properly motivated, but let's keep this PG rated, ok? My bosses are reading this.

George is a Midwesterner, comedian, actor, charmer, cigar-lover, and charismatic television and stage personality. He is a seasoned game show host, currently securing his spot in television history as the announcer for *The Price is Right* with Drew Carey on CBS. "I am certain Madonna's middle name is more famous than I am," said George. "But in the context of *The Price is Right*, it makes perfect sense to have me there. It's so much fun."

Everyone was thrilled to hear George was coming on board as a host for a weekend of live shows. Even though the touring show was successful and had been growing steadily for over a decade, there was always a bit of a gap between the television and live productions. Having the announcer from the television show as the host of the live show did a lot to cement the bond between the two entities. To the audience, the game show world is one big family. While George's shooting and appearance schedule doesn't allow for frequent dates on the road, he does make it to select cities a few times a year and the crowds always enjoy getting to see him live. "I *want* to do this. It's a perfect fit and a great way for the fans to get even closer to the action," said George. "It's cool to be on the other side of things."

Interestingly, the first two weekends I played the Mystic Lake Casino in Prior Lake, Minnesota, I worked with a new host. I heard that George had worked the show in Branson some time earlier, but my first time with him would be on the same stage I welcomed Pat Finn the previous year.

I really had no idea what to expect from George. I was certainly familiar with his work on *Price* and as the host of the syndicated version of *The Weakest Link*, but other than that, I didn't know what was in store for us.

As it happened, we were in store for a man who truly enjoys having a good time. He rivals Joey Fatone in the fun-having department, and he is great at making a room light up with energy and excitement. Whether he is on stage or off, he simply charges his surroundings with a buzzing sense that a good time is about to happen. I didn't know any of this at the time, nor did I know I would close out a bar to discover this.

When I first met George in Minnesota I was at the casino bar with our model, Amanda. He arrived with our executive producer dressed in a flamboyant red jacket. He was very obviously *not* one of the regular casino patrons, and looked every bit the television personality. People followed him throughout the casino and up to the bar. He posed for photos, signed autographs, and was as gracious as any of our hosts. Apparently, he had just completed a brief bit of promotional work for our show just moments before. I assumed it had been a scheduled affair, and was surprised to find out it was a lot more off-the-cuff. "Dude, I just got off a tiny platform stage with a local DJ spinning

"The Wobble" and I judged an impromptu dance contest in the lounge! Hi. I'm George."

It wasn't long before the entire gang was being entertained by George's stories and seemingly endless budget for drinks. He made sure that the night before we had to get down to business was filled with fun and frolic. One by one, the rest of the gang started making their way back to their rooms until only George and I remained. I kept thinking we were the set-up for a joke. "Two game show announcers walk into a bar . . ." I admit that George purchased more rounds than I did. Given that the only time I met his television counterpart, Drew Carey, I was also severely outgunned regarding the drinks, I settled into the fact that I simply wasn't going to be able to play Bar Tab Volley with George, and continued enjoying our conversation.

Like Todd Newton, George is a St. Louis area native. Like me, he has a stand-up comedy background. We talked like old friends, sharing stories about mutual friends in the business, comedy clubs we had both worked, cigars we enjoyed — it was possibly the quickest I have ever felt *that* comfortable with a host since I started the with the show.

Rehearsal the next day was an unusual affair. It was strange having the guy who says *Come On Down!* every day of the week on television there with us. Of course, there are enough little differences on stage compared to the television show that it made sense. "It is a little strange taking on Drew's role," Gray said. "At first, it felt a little like I was cheating on my wife."

Some of our set pieces are a tad smaller in scale then on the television production. It was interesting getting his perspective on the sets and other ways our show differed from his. When George saw the lectern I had to stand behind during the show, one considerably smaller than the announcer's booth he had on set at CBS, he took some time to offer a few jokes.

Working with George is very much like hanging out with him offstage. He is definitely a man who is out to have a good time. As a host, he tries to make every game, every moment onstage, a party. When he is first introduced, he rarely makes a graceful host's entrance through those famous doors. He'll time it so when the doors open, he'll appear to have been comically thrown on stage by a crew member. He won't go out into the crowd to shake a few hands in the center section. He'll run at full stride in his shiny coats and designer jeans out to the farthest reaches of the auditorium to find the person with the absolute worst seat in the house and share a moment. He strikes intentionally cheesy poses during jokes whether they do or don't hit with the crowd. He pokes fun at his outfits, his hair, and his jewelry. He hugs everyone as if they were long lost family, and shakes hands like he just lost a contest of strength. In short, he is the most animated of our hosts and he brings out wonderful responses from the crowd.

George definitely takes more of a comedian's approach to hosting than most of the others I have worked with. "I am a big fan of loose comedy," said George. He is very good at putting the contestants at ease, and everyone a moment to shine. "You have to *listen* to the contestants. Whether you are on *The Tonight Show*, *Good Morning America*, or a game show, the thing you have in common is you are interviewing someone and that's where the comedy lies." George continued, "The time to shine is when you can take what is happening with a real person in a real moment and have a great time with them." He also has a special appreciation for what it's like to be the announcer of a show, and that translated well into our interaction.

George does a commendable job of making me and the audience feel as though we have the same job, we just work in different offices. He takes time out of every show to discuss how many names we butcher before we say the three most famous words in game show history. We often banter back and forth, and on at least one occasion, have spontaneously burst into a "Dueling Announcer" routine. I rattled off random copy lines about a grocery item and he returned in kind with a different item. The routine would continue from item to item, prize to prize, and get faster, with cheesy game show goodness as we delivered every line. The bit reached its peak when we both shouted out "*A New Car!*" in unison. It wasn't a rehearsed thing, it was just a couple of comedians and announcers having a great time.

George makes certain everyone on that stage has an identity. He pointed out to me how when Drew Carey took over as host of *TPIR*, one thing he wanted to do was make certain the announcer and every model was known by name. It wasn't Drew asking for an item and a pretty girl bringing out a nice watch to display, it was "George, what is Manuela bringing out for the contestants to bid on." You heard this kind of language occasionally during the Barker years, but there was a more concerted effort to make it more of a prominent feature of the show when Drew took over. It gave the viewers someone to look forward to seeing on TV every day because it identified everyone on the show. George brings that practice to the stage. I've mentioned before how difficult it is making and maintaining a name for yourself in entertainment. Having someone so easily recognized by fans of the show working harder to make our identities more solid in the minds of the fans means a lot.

That sense of inclusion is not limited to the stage. If the venue provided a stocked bar or catering just for George, it soon became a bar and catering for the model and the announcer. If there was a meet and greet and someone brought George a drink to enjoy in between photos, we were all taken care of. If there was time for a cigar before or after the show, you can bet I was there smoking next to him. He's that generous, and wants everyone to enjoy the party.

It was that conversation with George Gray the first night we met that sparked the idea for this book. He had mentioned how Mark Walberg was such a good friend of his and helped him get work in Hollywood in the early days which made me think about Pat Finn, who came on board because of Walberg's recommendation as well. I thought about the stories I'd heard about Joey Fatone working with Drew Lachey, Todd Newton with Marc Summers, all the stories I'd heard about our producer, Jeff Palmer, working with JD Roberto, and how they met Andy Felsher on the same show, and then Andy hired me. In this business, everyone eventually knows and has worked with everyone else. Hearing George's many stories about people we had in common made me better appreciate the good fortune I had in landing (and keeping) this job. It's a small world and who knew where this one job would take me? Working with him, a direct descendant to the show that started it all, I was again reminded that I was involved with a truly special show.

....

George Gray On:

- **Being a Great Host**

I like somebody who is fast on their feet and who actually listens. It's truly the sign of a genius if you can listen and react well. You can't do it yourself. You need to listen to that other person on stage. It's just as much fun to learn about where someone is from and what they do as it is to watch them play the games. For me, those are the fun parts, the ones that have nothing to do with winning a prize. I try to keep things loose. I mean, know where you are, and where you have to go, but have fun along the way.

- **Strengths and Weaknesses**

I think I fill out a pair of slacks nicely. *Take that, Gene Rayburn! [laughs].* I think I am fast on my feet and very good at keeping things loose and relaxed. I am good at listening to the contestants. I think my weak point is that my ego won't allow me to believe I have any weak points [*laughs*].

- **The Contestants**

On *Weakest Link*, I was more like the friend who would laugh at you if you fell on a banana peel. I wouldn't want you to get hurt, but I would definitely make fun of you. On *Price*, everybody is in a great mood all the time. They are all there to see a show they grew up with. They're great.

- **The Nervous Contestants**

We had a guy on *Weakest Link*, a doctor, who froze so badly, he couldn't get the number of ribs in the human body correct. You just have to go with every moment and try to make everyone feel they're a part of that moment.

- **Not Being Bob Barker or Drew Carey**

I've never had that problem or seen it as a disadvantage. In fact, I see it as a total advantage. All of the guys who host game shows are total professionals and they all have a bigger name than I do. Because I am part of the television show, the Bob/Drew thing isn't a factor. It's probably the one time in my life where people would rather see me than Jerry Springer! [*laughs*]

- **Favorite Moments**

I just love watching people live out their dreams and enjoying a great moment on stage. It's the easiest show to do warm-up for. When I am on the television show, I am Santa Claus, or at least Santa's well-dressed elf. Santa has a big bag of presents for you, so how can you boo Santa Claus? Santa Claus is not the IRS.

- **Idols and Influences**

I grew up a big fan of loose comedy and comedians. I loved watching Benny Hill, Flip Wilson, Bob Newhart, Tim Conway and Harvey Korman. Now, I get to work on the stage where *The Carol Burnett Show* was taped. It's incredible.

George Gray can be seen every Monday through Friday as the announcer for The Price is Right on the CBS Television Network.

TWELVE

....

MARC SUMMERS

"*Wheel, Jeopardy,* and *Price* are the three game shows that are institutions, and you can't really screw around with them. More people came in to see the game than came in to see Marc Summers."

- Marc Summers

....

An argument could be made that next to Jerry Springer, Marc Summers is the most recognizable of all the hosts I have worked with over the years. "I've hosted twenty-five shows," Mark says. From starting out as the host of the wildly popular *Double Dare*, he has become a fixture on the Food Network, where he produces or hosts countless programs.

"I've probably done this thing as long as they've had it on the road," says Marc. "Back when they used to pay us a whole ton of dough [*sarcastic laughter*]. I did this in Las Vegas for a month, Atlantic City for three weeks, some casinos in Kansas City — It's a fun show to do. It's just fun to go out and do it!" As it happens, Marc's history with the world's greatest game show goes back rather a long way.

"I have known Bob Barker from the time I was 21 years old. I was a page on *Price* at CBS Television City," Summers said. "The first time I met him, I was bumbling [*laughs*]. Six or seven months later, I was hired as an idea man on *Truth or Consequences*. I got kind of close to him [*Barker*]."

Marc is the eleventh television host I have worked with so far, and I was genuinely excited to work with him. Being a big fan of the Food Network, and making frequent appearances on the network myself on *Mystery Diners*, just hearing that Marc was planning to host a show in Merrillville, Indiana was enough to get my heart racing.

I knew he was a fellow Midwesterner (He's from Indiana), and that we have similar backgrounds as comedians and variety performers. "I started out as a live performer," said Marc. "I was a magician and then I went into stand-up comedy. I put myself through college doing magic. I worked the Magic Castle from 1973 through 1981."

His comedy background shows well on stage. At one point in his career, he was referred to as The King of

Warm-Up because he had developed a reputation for being *the* go-to guy if you wanted the audience of your TV program to be revved up for the show. While still a page at CBS, he was called in from the page's lounge to do warm-up for *The Joker's Wild* with Jack Barry after the regular warm-up comedian couldn't make it to the show. "Soon it began to build my confidence, and I began doing warm-ups on sit-coms. Before you knew it I was doing *Soap, Star Search, Webster, Alice, What's Happening Now, Hour Magazine*. At one point, I was doing [*warm-up for*] *Soap*, the stage next to me had Bob Saget doing [*warm-up for*] *Bosom Buddies*, and the stage to the left of me was *Barney Miller*, where David Letterman was doing the warm-up on that.

I was not a fan of *Double Dare*, but that doesn't mean I didn't enjoy the show. By the time *DD* started taking over the world one bucket of slime at a time, I was already on the road with circuses and variety shows and rarely watched television. Most of my friends, however, were obsessed with the show. Prior to beginning another game show tour in 2014, I let a handful of my friends know I would be working with Marc. It was like I had told them I'd be working with Elvis Presley. The audiences at the Star Plaza were equally as enthused to see Marc take the stage.

As a host, Marc is a stone cold pro in every way. He personifies what most would expect from a game show host: he's funny, friendly, affable, and familiar to the audience. In some ways, he's a throwback to the last great era of game shows, but still maintains his credibility as being from the new generation of hosts.

Marc always appears in complete control, and runs the game with a laid back, demonstrative confidence. Of course, he admits that the live version of *Price* is the type of show where you can get by if the host manages to forget a rule or two. "Familiarity is the key," Marc said. "If I haven't hosted the show in some time and stumble on a rule, the fans will let me know right away because they know the game better than anyone." He also says that "They [CBS] have been very lucky with Drew Carey. The reality is, they cast someone who had never hosted a game show. Is Drew good at what he does? Apparently so, because people tend to watch the program. They say they have host-driven shows and shows where the host is somewhat irrelevant. I think this show is not as much host-driven, but if there was somebody there that America didn't like, they wouldn't stay tuned. He's obviously kicking ass and doing great. Does he understand the games? I'm not sure [*laughs*], but maybe that's irrelevant."

Having not hosted a live game show in some time, he told me he was going to rely on me for guidance in case he strayed from the path. "It's hard to screw it up," he said. "If I get it wrong, I am sure you know the show better than I do at this point." With a few minor hiccups, he led the show brilliantly and the audience, a home state crowd, was very happy to see him. "They paid good money to come in and with that in mind, I want them to feel they spent their money wisely and they were entertained."

He runs a modest-paced show and allows a lot of time for interaction between the host and the announcer. In fact, there were a few times we were required to stall in order to grant the stagehands enough time to move a game into place. He was quick to start a familial type conversation with me as opposed to just volley some back-and-forth game show banter, much like my encounters with JD Roberto. It's a nice way to tell the audience we are a team, and it gave the appearance that Summers and Martello had done this show together countless times before.

I am humbled by his support of my work. Marc and I worked together very well by my estimation and I was so pleased to hear him tell our executive producer how well he thought I did the job. "It's great having fresh blood with so much talent to draw upon," he said. "He's great!"

....

Marc Summers On:

- **Being A Great Host**

Bob [*Barker*] and I had a conversation once about what makes a great game show host. Both of us felt that Jack Benny was probably the best personality on television. Why? Because he made everybody else the star. He laid back and he reacted. Bob Barker was the king of reacting; he was great at it. If he got one great line a week, that was fine. He reacted to the people the best.

- **Strengths and Weaknesses**

I have tried to model my career around Barker, Jack Benny, and some of Johnny Carson. Their abilities to listen and make everyone else the star is what I was going for. If it's all about you, it doesn't work.

I do tend to get a little lazy after I have done a lot of shows and I find I don't always listen. I find I've asked Betty from Iowa her name three times and I just can't stay in the moment and remember Betty's name. When you do a large block of shows, three, four weeks at a time, you do zone out occasionally and start to think about where I will be doing my laundry in the next town. I get angry with myself whenever I get out of the zone. It may happen with all of us. I saw Carson occasionally zone out. Perhaps if a bit bombed, he didn't care. I *never* saw Barker off his game. I never saw Jack Benny phone it in.

- **The Contestants**

When you produce a lot of game shows, there is a saying which goes, "Contestants will find a way to screw you every time." This doesn't mean they're out to hurt you. They want to have fun, but they want to *win*. They're always looking for some little advantage they can use to facilitate winning. *Price* is almost foolproof. Everything is out in the open for them and the audience knows the games better than anyone. They'll tell you if something is not right. People mistakenly think if they come to several shows in a row, they'll see the same prizes or the same games. The producers of *Price* are kept well on their toes, and do a great job of keeping it fresh and fair.

- **The Nervous Contestants**

You know, the thing I try to do is make them feel comfortable. I'm a touchy-feely-huggy guy. So if I feel the nervousness, I put my arm around the guy or the girl and then I try to focus on them; find out about their lives.

- **The Drunk Contestants**

I saw a guy last night on videotape who was magical [*referring to a very drunk contestant with Todd Newton*]. You never ever, ever, ever, *ever* want to make fun of a contestant. I saw the drunk guy on the tape with Todd, and the audience was with Todd. He could have done anything and the audience would have laughed. The guy was good-spirited from drinking all of those good spirits. If there's a chance to do a little quip in the middle that isn't at their expense, I'll do it. But if I learned nothing else from Bob Barker, it was if you get the audience and the contestants to be angry and turn against you, you've lost control of the show, and that's the last thing that you want.

- **Not Being Bob Barker or Drew Carey**

The hardest part is dealing with the fact that everyone identifies with Barker. You want to stay true to it [*the game*], but you don't want to be Barker. I could do Barker. I could do the inflections . . . and sometimes I'll fall into it for the hell of it, but you have to make it your own. Because I've been on TV now for, God help me, thirty years, people know who I am via *Double Dare* and/or the Food Network stuff. So, I try to do a little cross section. I try to do a little homage to Bob, but I try to make it my own. I'm a little more playful. I've never really worried about it at all. I've been on TV long enough. When we played Kansas City last time, where Bob had his Barker's Beauties, I had a group of ladies, all fairly hot [*laughs*], who were wearing t-shirts that said Summers' Sweeties. You can't compete with the guy who owns the brand. I never went out there saying, "Oh, I'm going to show Bob how it's done."

- **Favorite Moments**

I'm always amazed people get excited about specific games. I celebrate in the joy and the excited feeling they get to have.

- **Idols and Influences**

Bob Barker, Jack Benny, and Johnny Carson were my biggest influences. Benny was a big influence because he got a joke with just a look or a take to the camera.

....

Marc Summers is a fixture on the Food Network as the host of Unwrapped, and is the executive producer of several popular programs, including Restaurant Impossible, Food Feuds, and Dinner Impossible.

THIRTEEN

....

THE HOSTS' HOST

The Price is Right LIVE! continues to sell out venues across North America. Even though it is a show many don't even realize exists until they hear the advertisements for it on the radio or television, it proudly carries on the television fun that started with Bill Cullen in the 1950s, became a piece of Americana with Bob Barker in the 1970s, and found new life in the mid-2000s with Drew Carey.

The hosts I have worked with on that show, each with their own unique styles and abilities, are the torch-bearers for the Olympic Marathon run the original show continues to enjoy. They carry on the tradition of television's most exciting hour of fabulous prizes to theaters, arenas, and casino stages several times a year to the delight of untold thousands of screaming spectators. Game show magic is on display, and bucket list dreams are fulfilled with the utterance of a single phrase. These talented hosts are there to receive every hug and kiss along the way.

For me, I continue to learn from these greats and admire their obvious skills and limitless abilities. Hosting is something I have always yearned to do. I continue to prepare and present pitches for television programs with the hopes I may one day sell an idea and, better yet, host the show.

In my 30+ years in entertainment, I always thought I had what it takes to do the job. After all, I have performed for a President of the United States, sung the blues with Buddy Guy playing guitar behind me, been directed by Robert Altman, and even told Audrey Hepburn she was "one classy broad." I must have some chops, right? After watching these eleven men do what they do best, I realized that I was not at all close to being the guy holding the mic, sitting behind a desk, or asking America to guess the price without going over. Thankfully, as a result of the best gig I've ever had, I feel as though I have been treated to a Master Class taught by Suma Cum Laude graduates and PhD level professors . . . and I was actually *paid* to do it. I may never be the guy hosting the show, but truthfully, if I were the guy saying *"Come on Down!"* on stage for the rest of my life, it wouldn't bother me one bit. If nothing else, I would have a better feeling that I indeed have the job. What would be even better is knowing I would continue to meet, befriend, and work with some truly incredible hosts. I may not be famous, but thanks to these people, I always feel like a star.

This final question was asked to the hosts primarily for fun. I expected it to be taken about as seriously as "what kind of tree would you be?" Instead, it turned out to be a favorite, and in some cases, the most difficult to answer. I found the responses fascinating. In many ways, they were representative of the hosts' personalities and approaches to their jobs

"Living or dead, in show business or not, who would you like to see hosting *The Price is Right* or a live game show?"

- **Mark Walberg:** Tough question. One of my favorites is Jimmy Kimmel. I'd love to watch him because he would butcher the show for his own amusement.
- **Bob Goen:** My *God*, what a question! If I am going completely off the board and I'm not obligated to pick a game show host, I have to go with Albert Brooks. When I first started at *Entertainment Tonight* they said "Give us a list of who I wanted to interview", and I had a one-name list. He's the only man I ever wanted to meet! He'd bring the show to a whole different level.
- **Joey Fatone:** William Shakespeare!
- **Todd Newton:** *Johnny Carson!* Without a doubt. But, you know, this is a tough question.

You really have to ask yourself, "Do I want to see a great host *of The Price is Right,* or do I want to see someone great *hosting The Price is Right?"* I could also see picking someone off the wall for fun. Johnny was the king. What he could have done with *Price* . . . What did the other guys say?

- **Jerry Springer:** Who would make a great host? Let me see, if it couldn't be me, probably Jerry Seinfeld *or* Don Rickles. They're, obviously, both, in different ways, so incredibly talented. I mean, *those* people are talented! Rickles is just so fast. Seinfeld is such a great observer of human behavior. He would be picking up things from our contestants that I am not getting and he would get it like that [*snaps fingers*]. So those guys would be so entertaining. Of course, I'd like to see those guys going to the grocery store commenting on what they get from aisle seven and why.
- **JD Roberto:** A woman, definitely. Women get very few chances to host game shows. There are notable exceptions, to be sure, but exceptions nonetheless. I'd like to see how the dynamic would change with a woman on the microphone. I'd be thrilled to announce for Ellen Degeneres.
- **Dave Ruprecht:** I hate to be boring, but that would be Todd Newton. He is just head and

shoulders above the rest of us, including me. I don't think I'd want a non-host [*to take on the role*] because it is just so much harder than we make it look.

- **Pat Finn:** This is such a hard question. There are so many ways you can go with this. I would say from an audience perspective, the most exciting choice would have to be Bob Barker. What a delight it would be to see him on the live stage. If I am going completely off the wall, Robin Williams. Can you imagine what he would have done with the show? Such a great talent. I'm also a big fan of Jimmy Fallon. You know, I don't know the right answer. [*laughs*]

- **George Gray:** *Really?* Oh Man!

- **Marc Summers:** Oh, *Wow!* Bob [*Goen*] said Albert Brooks? Really? [*laughs*] It's a different question because, do you want to see somebody turn it into a different program or do you want to keep what it is? The first person that comes to mind is Ryan Seacrest. Ryan does not get the credit he deserves. When we were working on a program called *Ultimate Revenge*, I'd say, "I need nineteen seconds for the close, you want me to count you down?" He'd go over into the corner and say, "Give me a few minutes. I could do it." He'd give me nineteen seconds on the nose. The only other person I saw do that was Bob Barker. Barker was the king of that. When I was a page [for *The Price is Right*], I'd say to him, "We've got twelve seconds," and he'd do it. Twenty-two seconds, forty-two seconds . . . He got it every time. Ryan can do that. Ryan has studied Dick Clark, Merv Griffin, myself — he is a consummate host and a classy guy. He's probably the closest to Barker. Some people say he doesn't have a sense of humor. I disagree. I think he'd have to be a tad looser than I normally see him, but, I think if you want to go back to old school that would be my choice. Ryan is an old guy in a young person's body.

SPECIAL THANKS

Many thanks go to my supportive family.
Marty Martello and Mary Morrison Martello, Chris, Emily,
Gemma, Lisa and Randy Hayward, Will, Jed and Cori,
Matt Martello, Nick and John Martello,
April Sperk, Sue Sperk, and Samantha McKie.

To the OTHER incredible people I have worked with at *The
Price is Right LIVE!* I offer my sincerest apologies to anyone
I have inadvertently left off of this list.
Cathy Dawson, Jeff Palmer, Andy Felsher, who, *eventually,*
gave me my favorite job in show business.
Brandon Huff, Clint Montgomery, Deinna Charee,
Marilyn Saidman, Melonie Harrison Santos, Ivan Copelan,
Lauren Siefer, Jeffrey Mensch, Kristen Urban, Mike Bevans,
Amanda Langlais, Debbie Stieglitz, Rachel Hall, Lauren Darcy
Adabashi, Ashlé Worrick, Lauren Osmond, Dominika Zybko,
Markie McManus, Amie Nicole, Rachel Day. Jay Silva,
Adam Dexter, Sarah Walker, Corey Kloos, Em Weathers,
Lou Cavallari, Susan Hurst, Kyle Hays, James Chief-Yepa,
Todd Whitaker, Geoffery Bernardi, Krista Meadows,
Jesse Cosens, J.R. Roberson, Mike Navage, Maria Bermudez
Stacey Scarborough, Sam Schwartz, Lisa Weinshrot,
Joel Foster, Chris Donnan, Shauna O'Brien, Adam Lee,
Luis Hermosillo, Mitch Kellman, Allen Sowersby,
David Streator, Mark Gigas (and Gypsy), Clay Scott,
and the crews at the Jubilee and Lawrence Welk Theaters.

HERE'S YOUR ANNOUNCER!

Andy Martello is an award-winning author, entertainer, and comedian.
Originally from Chicago, he now makes his home in
Las Vegas, Nevada.

You have seen his television work on *American Restoration*, *Mystery
Diners*, *Last Comic Standing*, and *Street Genius* (aka *None of the Above*).
In 2016, he was named Best Local Author by the
Las Vegas Review-Journal in their annual Best of Las Vegas poll.

His first book, *The King of Casinos: Willie Martello and the El Rey Club* has
earned 14 prestigious awards, including an
International Book Award, a Book Excellence Award,
a Readers' Favorite Book Award, and a
USA Best Books Award for best biography.
It is currently in development to become a major motion picture.

When reviewing this book on Amazon, please look for Andy's other
works which include *The King of Casinos*, *Pretty Words. Nothing More.*, and
Andy Martello's Stupid Stories About Famous People.

Future books include *Andy Martello's The Roommate Chronicles* and the
poetry books *Pretty Words. So Much More.*, and *The Broken Mirror*.

Website: andymartello.com   Email: andy@andymartello.com
Facebook: facebook.com/andymartelloentertainment
Twitter: twitter.com/THEandymartello
Goodreads: goodreads.com/AndyMartello

9 780997 045628